THE GUINNESS HITS CHALLENGE 2

QUIZ MASTERS

TIM RICE
MIKE READ
JO RICE
PAUL GAMBACCINI

GUINNESS BOOKS

ACKNOWLEDGEMENTS

The four authors would like to thank the following for their help
and cooperation: Judy Craymer, Eileen Heinink, Fay
Rawlinson, Jan Rice, *New Musical Express*, *Melody Maker* and
Music Week

Editorial: Beatrice Frei, John English and Sheila Goldsmith

Layout and Design: David Roberts and Sheila Goldsmith

First edition 1984
Second edition 1985

© **GRRR Books Ltd and Guinness Superlatives Ltd 1985**

Published in Great Britain by Guinness Superlatives Ltd
33 London Road, Enfield, Middlesex

British Library Cataloguing in Publication Data

Guinness hits challenge. – 2nd ed.
   1. Music, Popular (Songs, etc.) – Miscellanea
   I. Rice, Jo
   780'.42'076   ML3470

   ISBN 0–85112–466–6

Filmset by Fakenham Photosetting Ltd, Fakenham, Norfolk
Printed and bound in Great Britain by
Dotesios (Printers) Ltd., Bradford-on-Avon, Wiltshire

INTRODUCTION

What? A second *Hits Challenge*? What possible reason is there for causing even more headaches to the thousands of people who tried – sometimes successfully – to match up to the first *Hits Challenge*? Is it just a hankering for more money after the gratifying success of the first book?

Well, yes and no. *Hits Challenge* is proving to be a lot of fun to compile, even if we can't always answer each other's questions. The response to the 'More Questions Than Answers' section in the first book was strong enough to encourage us to hit you all with another 100 questions in the certain knowledge that we will not have to give away too many future editions of *British Hit Singles* to those of you who score 100%. The money the book earned us, though, was not enough to allow us all to retire before we write a few more.

Retire? There's no chance of that for a year or two, not while there's a singles chart and an albums chart every week, and a popular music industry to statisticize, annotate and ask questions about, not to mention to listen to and enjoy.

This book serves up questions at a cost of roughly seven for a penny, which is the sort of deal you don't meet every day. It's the kind of bargain that makes you want to start saving now for *Hits Challenge 3*.

PAUL GAMBACCINI

MIKE READ

TIM RICE

JO RICE

Directors, Grrr Books Ltd

Scoring System

The questions in section A of each quiz are, in the opinions of the authors at least, easier than those in section B which in turn are easier than the real toughies in section C. We suggest you award yourself one point for each correct answer to an

A question, two points for scores in a B situation, and three for the ultimate triumph of a C bullseye, unless of course the introduction to the quiz indicates to the contrary.

<table>
<tr><td>QUIZ 1</td><td>WHERE ARE YOU NOW (MY LOVE)</td></tr>
</table>

The answers to all these clues are places – towns, countries, streets, rivers, oceans, continents or planets. Many are song titles, some are not.

1 Where Frankie Goes To
2 Where Murray Head spent one night
3 Where Alphaville are big
4 Tears For Fears thought it was Mad, but Everybody Wants To Rule it
5 Band Aid want to feed it, USA for Africa are it
6 Where David Bowie's 1983 girl came from
7 Where Elbow Bones and the Racketeers were taken for one night
8 What the Rah Band saw clouds across
9 Instrumentally, this country didn't cry for the Shadows
10 Gerry and Frankie both ferried across this river
11 Sham 69 were boys from here
12 Sea of Billy Ocean's queen
13 Ultravox's European capital
14 Where Kenny Ball and his Jazzmen played at Midnight
15 Town where I'm in love with the girl on a certain megastore checkout desk
16 Where Max Bygraves will bring tulips from
17 Adam and the Ants serenaded the young people of this city
18 Eagles' hotel
19 Where Kim Wilde's kids are
20 Where Bruce Springsteen says he was born

1 Buck's Fizz town
2 Where Jam's rifles went to school?
3 Toto's continent
4 Where Men At Work's second hit came from
5 Where Police walked to number one
6 What Police found invisible at number two
7 Suzi Quatro's demon town
8 Human League's war-torn country

9   Where Sal Solo's Heart and Soul are

10 Electric Light Orchestra didn't miss this train

11 Where Fiddler's Dram went on a day trip

12 Are there Piranhas in this river?

13 Captain Sensible's suburb

14 The state that wanted R. Dean Taylor

15 The state whose bluebird took a message to Martha in 1964

16 Wings' old country, sir

17 City whose cathedral brought the New Vaudeville Band down

18 City of Redbone's witch queen

19 Where the 'Seven Drunken Nights' hitmakers came from

20 Where Ossie dreamed Spurs were on their way to

1   Donovan's tube station B-side

2   King Kurt's 1983 destination

3   Cliff Richard's Little Town

4   Video Symphonic's TV theme about this region's flame trees

5   Tommy Steele's Kenyan city

6   The state in which John Denver reached his Rocky Mountain High

7   Town around which the Sloop John B, and my grandaddy and me, sailed

8   Where Charlie Daniels said Johnny met the Devil

9   Sub-title of Des O'Connor's 'Dick-A-Dum-Dum'

10 River that John Leyton went down

11 Bridge on which Simon and Garfunkel were feeling groovy

12 Town where Lonnie Donegan spent five weeks in jail in 1959

13 Town that Glen Campbell sang about once he'd finished with Phoenix and Wichita

14 Alan Price sang of this North East town

15 Where Marty Robbins shot a man in Rose's cantina

16 Where the Temperance Seven followed up 'You're Driving Me Crazy'

17 Where Brook Benton and Randy Crawford both spent rainy nights

18 Sea across which the Goons walked backwards for Christmas

19 Bobby Bloom's Caribbean holiday resort

20 Where Johnny Horton went north to

A LITTLE BIT OF SOAP

Score one point for each correct answer.
All questions refer to your favourite TV Soap Operas.

1 He played Len Fairclough's nephew in *Coronation Street* before going on to top the charts (with his group) on both sides of the Atlantic

2 For a while *Crossroads* used an alternative version of their theme tune. Who recorded it?

3 They had a hit in 1979 with 'I Don't Want To Be A Freak' and minor hits in '80 and '83 with 'I've Just Begun To Love You' and 'Does That Ring A Bell'

4 Group of 'boys' who were TV favourites in the late 50s, often appearing on *Oh Boy*

5 In 1963 *Coronation Street*'s Dennis Tanner managed pop singer Walter Potts in the serial. Potts had a hit featured in several episodes. Under what name and what was the hit?

6 Who played Ena Sharples' grandson in *Coronation Street* before making it big in a group that was heralded as "America's answer to the Beatles"?

7 *Dr. Kildare* star Richard Chamberlain took which Elvis Presley song into the Top 20?

8 What is the link between Elvis Presley and Dallas?

9 What is the link between Simon May, Stephanie de Sykes and Kate Robbins?

10 Which singer first appeared as Johnny St. Cyr in the 60s serial *Harper's West One* singing his new record which subsequently went to number one?

<table>
<tr><td>QUIZ 3</td><td># LIVING IN THE PAST</td></tr>
</table>

This is the first of quizzes about specific years. This one goes back the furthest – to 1959 – the year that Paul Gambaccini first heard about Cliff Richard.

Who had the big UK hits with these titles:

1 'Chantilly Lace'
2 'It Doesn't Matter Anymore'
3 'Donna'
4 'The Day The Rains Came'
5 'Smoke Gets In Your Eyes'
6 'Problems'
7 'I Got Stung'
8 'A Big Hunk O' Love'
9 'Roulette'
10 'Kiss Me Honey Honey Kiss Me'
11 'It's Late'
12 'Dream Lover'
13 'Living Doll'
14 'A Teenager In Love'
15 'I've Waited So Long'
16 'What Do You Want To Make Those Eyes At Me For'
17 'What Do You Want'
18 'High Hopes'
19 'Red River Rock'
20 'Rawhide'

1 The man who started 1959 in the number one slot went on to become one of the most popular country singers of all time during the 70s and 80s. One of his other '59 pop hits was a rock revival of a Nat King Cole standard. Who is he?
2 What major event in rock history took place on 3 February 1959?
3 Which instrumental aggregation featured a well-known writer and broadcaster on tenor sax? They had one enormous hit and one lesser one.
4 Which instrumentalist enjoyed 79 chart weeks in 1959, more than any other act?

5   What instrumental combo was led by Johnny Paris?

6   Which major UK female recording artiste had two singles in the top three in February?

7   And which of those two singles made number one?

8   Who had the lesser UK hit with 'Battle Of New Orleans'?

9   Which femme who had had five simultaneous chart entries in 1955 made her last chart appearance in 1959?

10 Who took Brecht and Weill to number one?

11 Why was 1959 a good year for Trevor Stanford?

12 And why was it good for Terence Perkins?

13 And why was it a little disappointing for Sam Cooke?

14 Who burst into the charts for the first time with a Top Three single which was featured in a movie about a rock and roller joining the army? An EP from the movie also hit the Top 20 singles charts.

15 Who announced the arrival of summer when summer was all but over?

16 Which Lonely Boy wrote a chart-topper for Buddy Holly?

17 Who took Peter Gunn into the Top Ten?

18 Why was it ironic that Marty Wilde's 'Sea Of Love' was on the Philips label?

19 Who was 'that soldier boy'?

20 Which 1926 song gave Little Richard his most successful UK chart record?

1   How did Stonewall Jackson anticipate ABBA?

2   Who made his US chart debut with 'The Diary'?

3   How did Thomas Wayne anticipate the Bee Gees?

4   Which hit began "What would people say, what would people do"?

5   Who had a thing for Tall Paul?

6   Which British bandleader had a Top 20 hit in the US with 'The Children's Marching Song'?

7   Who took the title song of a Lerner/Loewe score into the British Top Ten?

8   What was unique about 1959 as far as Elvis Presley's recording career was concerned?

9   What was the achievement of the album *South Pacific* in 1959?

10 Who shared lead vocals with Frank Sinatra on a big 1959 single and then went on to have two minor solo UK hits in 1961 and 1962?

11 What was Slim Dusty's problem?

12 From what TV series did Ed "Kookie" Byrnes emerge?

13 Who wrote a book called *Twixt Twelve and Twenty*?

14 Which tiger roared up the US charts on several occasions in 1959 but merely whimpered in the UK Top 50 the following year?

15 Which 1959 number one US song (number one in the UK in 1960 by a different act) was alleged to have been nicked from the 1926 composition 'In A Little Spanish Town'?

16 Which composer/bandleader took *Peter Gunn* to the top of the US album charts?

17 Who had a Happy Organ?

18 Who sang a song about a Cadillac and a little Nash Rambler? (The act re-recorded the song for the British market without the automobile names)

19 Which song gave Carl Dobkins Jr his first and greatest brush with fame?

20 Who supported Don Lang?

| QUIZ 4 | C'MON AND SWIM |

This quiz is about water, whether in brooks, rivers, seas or streams. On some occasions bodies of water will be referred to by name.

1 Who piloted the 'Ferry Across The Mersey'?

2 What member of Chic co-produced Duran Duran's 'The Wild Boys'?

3 Who enjoys seasonal airplay with 'I Believe In Father Christmas'?

4 What heavy metal group noticed 'Smoke On The Water'?

5 What Dutch artist sailed into the UK Top Ten in 1981 with 'Caribbean Disco Show'?

6 In what song did Elvis Costello mention the River Mersey, Thames and Tyne?

7 What female vocalist emerged from Vinegar Joe to score solo hits under the direction of Lieber and Stoller?

8 Who enjoyed a number one album with *Atlantic Crossing*?

9 What was Queen's first hit?

10 Who made a comeback in 1984 with 'Caribbean Queen'?

11 What billed artist did not perform on Phil Spector's production 'River Deep Mountain High'?

12 Who reached the Top Ten in 1980 with 'Waterfalls'?

13 What was the flip side of Boney M's 'Brown Girl In The Ring'?

14 What was Creedence Clearwater Revival's colourful stream?

15 The Honeydrippers successfully revived which Phil Phillips and Marty Wilde hit?

16 'Bridge Over Troubled Water' by Simon and Garfunkel was number one in what year?

17 Kim Wilde's 1981 double-sided hit paid tribute to 'Boys'. What was the other title?

18 With whom did the Four Tops have a successful cover of 'River Deep Mountain High'?

19 Who had the number one version of 'Moon River'?

20 Bruce Springsteen's first two British hits were from which LP?

1 What Bobby Darin hit is also known by its French title 'La Mer'?

2 On what Elton John LP did 'Crazy Water' appear?

3 Who had an American number one with 'Poor Side Of Town'?

4 What was Tommy Steele's repetitious 1957 Top Five title?

5 What was Bob Dylan watching the river do?

6 What family group made their UK chart debut with 'Down By The Lazy River'?

7 Johnny and the Hurricanes sailed into the Top Three in 1959 with what rocker?

8 What was the Doobie Brothers' wet US number one?

9 What dance music star fronted a group called the Partners and then joined One Way?

10 In what song did Marvin Gaye assure Tammi Terrell there was no river wide enough to keep them apart?

11 Who was the Undertones' watery girl?

12 What American star was in the UK Top Thirty 'Endlessly'?

13 Who paddled 'Up On Cripple Creek'?

14 Who sang 'Many Rivers To Cross' in the film *The Harder They Come*?

15 In what did Styx sail?

16 Who complained there were 'Too Many Rivers'?

17 What duo left the Strawbs and quickly scored a Top Ten hit?

18 The theme of what ocean disaster film gave Maureen McGovern a US number one?

19 Who reached number two in 1961 with 'Lazy River'?

20 Who cruised up the 'Mississippi' to number one in 1976?

1 Who had the British hit with 'Wade In The Water'?

2 What famed bluesman's song helped inspire the name of the Rolling Stones?

3 On what label did the Detroit Spinners' number one 'Working My Way Back To You' appear?

4 In what pond did the Cowsills take a 1968 dip?

5 What supergroup navigated the 'Sea Of Joy'?

6 Who wore 'Warpaint' in the Top Ten in 1961?

7 When they left Motown in 1973 their first single was 'Where Peaceful Waters Flow'. Who were they?

8 What Standells classic appears on the album *Nuggets*?

9 What country and western great reached the Top Twenty with 'Sea Of Heartbreak'?

10 The piano figure from what Pat Boone hit was used in the background of Big Daddy's 'Dancing In The Dark'?

11 What Top Three Ken Dodd hit was an adaptation of 'Le Colline Sono In Fioro'?

12 Who scored a Top Forty hit with 'Can't You Hear My Heart'?

13 What was Joe Simon drowning in?

14 Two artists reached the Top Forty in 1977 with 'The Water Margin'. Name one of them

15 Who donned 'A Sky Blue Shirt And A Rainbow Tie' in the 1954 charts?

16 Who got to number two in America staring at the 'Allegheny Moon'?

17 What was the Rockin' Berries desperate plight?

18 Where did Neil Young shoot his beloved?

19 Who harmonized on the doo wop classic 'Over The Mountain; Across The Sea'?

20 Who floated 'Down The River Nile'?

<table>
<tr><td>QUIZ 5</td><td># YOU'RE MORE THAN A NUMBER IN MY LITTLE RED BOOK</td></tr>
</table>

This quiz concerns songs with numbers. All you have to do to earn your one, two or three points, is to give the correct number. Guessing could well earn you a point or two, since the answer must be a number of some magnitude.

1 Which century did T. Rex's 'boy' belong to?

2 How many tears did Question Mark cry?

3 How many times did Suzi Quatro crash?

4 How many eyes did Bobby Vee's night have?

5 Prince partied like it was which year?

6 Which Apollo took Adam Ant for a ride into the Top Ten?

7 What was the number of the Searchers' legendary love potion?

8 Which time around did Shalamar have their third hit?

9 On which plane were Saxon's 'Strangers In The Night' travelling?

10 Jimmy Pursey's 'Sham'?

11 How many Seas Of Rhye did Queen sail?

12 How many did Dave Brubeck take?

13 Manfred Mann's chart debut countdown?

14 How many steps beyond did Madness go?

15 How many guns did the Alarm fire?

16 How many times out of 10 was Cliff Richard unsuccessful?

17 What hours did Sheena Easton's baby work?

18 What was the number of the car belonging to Driver 67?

19 What was the number of David Bowie's T.V.C.?

20 Who did the Boomtown Rats look after?

1 The date of the Damned's Friday?

2 How many teens did Sweet sing about?

3 How many did Richard Myhill discover it took to tango?

4 The Purple Hearts reckoned there were how many like us?

5 How old was the Regents' girl?

6 How many miles did the Pretenders travel during Christmas '83?

7 Her hit EP contained how many from Toyah?

8 On which Century label were most of Barry White's hits?

9 What time did The Who's quadraphonic train run?

10 How many stars did Ruby Wright sing about?

11 Neil Sedaka last reigned in the chart in 1975 with the queen of which year?

12 How many people in Leo Sayer's band?

13 How many of Bob Marley's little birds were there?

14 How many strong winds blew Neil Young into the chart?

15 How many tears did the Goombay Dance Band cry?

16 What was Genesis's multiplications EP of 1982?

17 How many did Marvin Gaye and Kim Weston reckon it would take?

18 How many stars did Billy Fury sing about?

19 December of which year provided the Four Seasons with a number one?

20 How many pounds of clay did Craig Douglas have in 1961?

1 Number of the Brothers Johnson's strawberry letter?

2 How many little fingers did Frankie McBride have in 1967?

3 How many inches of rock did T. Rex chart in 1968?

4 How many did the Quads say there must be?

5 Where did Tight Fit go back to for their first hit?

6 With which year would you associate 'Exordium and Terminus'?

7 Which man gave the Shadows a hit in 1982?

8 How many Dam-nations went to the scarlet party?

9 Who was Peter Waterman in 1975?

10 How many lads were 'Standing On The Corner'?

11 What was the number of Roger Miller's engine?

12 According to Medicine Head how many is one and one?

13   In which year were Peter Jay and the Jaywalkers doing the 'Can Can'?

14   In which year did the Human League take a holiday?

15   Which street bridge song, written by Paul Simon, was a hit for Harper's Bizarre?

16   Which group were initially homicidal then obsessed?

17   In which class did Spencer Davis travel in 1968?

18   How many yellow roses did Bobby Darin have?

19   What time was it by Chicago's watch?

20   How many brothers sang about green fields?

QUIZ 6	PEOPLE ARE PEOPLE

This is a quiz about people and songs with similar names.

What surname matches all these first names?

1   Carly, Paul and Tito

2   Donny, Marie and Little Jimmy

3   Anita, Emmylou and Rolf

4   Smokey, Tom and Floyd

5   Hurricane, O.C. and Whistling Jack

6   Freddie, Kay and Ringo

7   Shakin', Cat and Ray

8   Al, Amii and Rod

9   Andy, Deniece and Mason

10   Paul, Jimmy and Faron

What song title have each of the following hit with?

11   Barbra Streisand and Frankie Laine

12   Demis Roussos and Slik

13   Tab Hunter and Donny Osmond

14   Rosemary Clooney and Shakin' Stevens

15   Eddie Calvert and Perez Prado

16   Harry Belafonte and Boney M

17   Platters and Flying Pickets

18   Elvis Presley, Frank Sinatra and Sex Pistols

19   Petula Clark and Harry Secombe

20   Crazy World of Arthur Brown and the Pointer Sisters

What surname matches all these first names?

1 Chuck, Mike and Dave
2 Tommy, Sonny and Rick
3 Adrian, LaVern and Ginger
4 R. Dean, Felice and James
5 Brian, J. Frank and Jackie
6 Jeff, John and Len
7 Carla, Rufus and B.J.
8 James, Joe and Arthur
9 Cliff, Tony and Boyd
10 Larry, Maurice and Hank

What song title have each of the following hit with?

11 Chris Farlowe, Aretha Franklin, Brenda Lee
12 Billie Davis, Exciters, Hello
13 Ella Fitzgerald, Louis Armstrong, King Kurt
14 Kool and the Gang, Boomtown Rats, Shirley Bassey
15 Elvis Presley, Stan Freberg, Jacksons
16 Belle Stars, Dixie Cups, Natasha
17 Dave Newman, Tight Fit, Tokens
18 Kathy Kirby, Ruby Murray, Joan Weber
19 Everly Brothers, Little Richard, Kenny Rogers
20 Anthony Newley, Donny Osmond, Bronski Beat

What surname matches all these first names?

1 Don, Ray, Tina
2 Edwin, Ronnie and Dale
3 Joe, Mick and Chuck
4 Arthur, Brenda and Peggy
5 Frankie, Roger and Steve
6 Bruce, David and Jimmy
7 Bill, Sandy and Willie
8 Don, Phil and Bryan
9 Tom, Paul and Jimmy
10 Jack, Linda and Simon

What song title have each of the following hit with?

11   Dave Berry, Connie Francis and Genesis
12   Temptations, Rod Stewart and Madness
13   Anita Bryant, Kaye Sisters and Marie Osmond
14   Dave Dee, Dozy, Beaky, Mick and Tich, Silver Convention and Queen
15   Santana, UK Subs and Zombies
16   Earth Wind and Fire, Nazareth and Kiki Dee
17   Ben E. King, John Lennon and Kenny Lynch
18   Four Tops, K.C. and the Sunshine Band and the Weathermen
19   Slim Whitman, Karl Denver and Ray Stevens
20   David Essex, T. Rex and Kelly Marie

| QUIZ 7 | SWEDISH RHAPSODY |

These questions are all about Super-Swedes ABBA, either as a group or as individuals.

1   Why ABBA?
2   Give the Christian and surnames of all four members of ABBA – spelling must be correct!
3   What song rocketed ABBA into the big time in 1974?
4   And in what circumstances was their first hit launched?
5   Which three acts have had more UK number ones than ABBA?
6   What record label released ABBA records in the UK?
7   Which of the following was *not* a number one in the UK – 'Fernando', 'Money Money Money', 'Dancing Queen', 'Mamma Mia'?
8   Which of the following was a number one in the UK – 'I Have A Dream', 'Chiquitita', 'Take A Chance On Me', 'S.O.S.'?
9   Who produced all of ABBA's recordings?
10   Which member of ABBA was married to Frida?
11   Which Swedish city was celebrated in 'Summer Night City'?
12   Which member of ABBA wrote the lyrics for the majority of their hits?

13 Which member of ABBA plays guitar as his principal instrument?

14 What is a Super Trouper?

15 What is the name of the musical written by the two ABBA writers, together with Tim Rice, first heard as a double album in late 1984?

16 Why are the group palindromic?

17 And mnemonic?

18 Who recorded the number one hits 'Figaro' and 'Angelo' which could conceivably have been inspired by 'Fernando'?

19 Which two ABBA hit titles consisted of the same word repeated three times?

20 Which member of ABBA was actually born in Norway?

1   What was ABBA's only US number one single?

2   What is the name of ABBA's manager (he also contributed to the writing of some of their early material)?

3   Which ABBA hit was covered by Blancmange in 1984, attaining a chart position 10 places higher than the original version?

4   Which song gave the two male ABBA members their tenth UK number one as writers and producers, an unequalled feat?

5   And who sang the song?

6   What is the name of ABBA's record company, label and recording studio?

7   Who produced Frida's first post-ABBA solo album?

8   Who produced Agnetha's first post-ABBA solo album?

9   Which country was the location for ABBA's movie?

10 Which charity were the royalties earned by 'Chiquitita' given to?

11 Which ABBA lyric mentions Marilyn French?

12 Which ABBA lyric mentions Glasgow?

13 Who had a hit in 1974 with ABBA song 'Honey Honey'?

14 Which was ABBA's only double-sided UK hit?

15 Which is the only ABBA UK A-side to feature male lead vocals?

16 Which ABBA hit repeated the same phrase five times over in the title?

17 What was the title of the "mini-musical" featured on *ABBA – The Album* consisting of three songs, billed as "three scenes from a mini musical"?

18 One of the songs from the mini-musical became one of ABBA's best-known compositions, but their version was not released as a single until 1983. Title, please.

19 What connection has Eric Stewart of 10 C.C. with ABBA?

20 What 18-record sequence did 'Head Over Heels' break in the UK?

1   Name the engineer of all ABBA's recordings

2   Which is the only song recorded by ABBA which, in its English Language version, credits, in addition to ABBA members and their manager, two other writers?

3   And who are those two other (well-known American) writers?

4   What ABBA flip side title is the same as the first name of an artist who has had a huge hit with another song with music written by ABBA members?

5   With which song did ABBA fail to reach the Eurovision finals in 1973?

6   What is the title of the only ABBA-written song to have been recorded by Frida since ABBA's (we hope temporary) break-up at the end of 1982?

7   Name the Swedish hit groups that the two male ABBA members played in

8   Which musical (Swedish stage production) featured Agnetha in a leading role in the early seventies?

9   What was Britain's entry (artiste and song) the year that ABBA won the Eurovision Song Contest?

10 In which country was it estimated that one household in three owned a copy of *ABBA – The Album*?

11 What is the connection between Agnetha and Glenn Frey?

12 Which American recording artist had a number four US hit with a song that had the same title as one of ABBA's biggest hits, and what was the title?

13 Which ABBA lyric includes a misuse of the word "since"?

14 What has Lasse Wellander contributed to ABBA records over the years?

15 What is the relevance of 'Conociendome, Conociendote' to ABBA?

16 Which three traditional American songs did ABBA record as a medley in 1976?

17 Which ABBA song started life as "Happy Hawaii"?
18 Which ABBA number one reappeared in a live version as the flip of 'I Have A Dream'?
19 What was ABBA's label in the United States?
20 How many UK chart singles had ABBA the group enjoyed by March 1985?

| QUIZ 8 | A BEATLE I WANT TO BE |

Questions about the Fab Four.

1 Who wanted a Beatle for Christmas?
2 Who were the Prefab Four?
3 In which song did the Beatles sing about B. B. King and Matt Busby?
4 What is the link between Hot Chocolate, Mary Hopkin and Badfinger?
5 Who first produced the Beatles in Hamburg?
6 What was the Beatles' first hit of their own on the Apple label?
7 Who used the name the "Nurk Twins" when performing together for fun?
8 What is the link between Shirley Bassey, Steve Harley and Olivia Newton John?
9 In which film did John Lennon play the part of a soldier?
10 In the song 'Glass Onion' who was the walrus?

1 Which group auditioned for Decca Records on the same day as the Beatles – 1 January 1962?
2 Who released a single on the Colpix label called 'A Beatle I Want To Be'?
3 What occurred on 1 August 1971?
4 When Ringo Starr was taken ill prior to a Beatles world tour, which former member of Georgie Fame's Blue Flames deputized and which group did he subsequently form?
5 What was the first instrumental the Beatles ever recorded?
6 Apart from the Polydor re-release of 'Ain't She Sweet', only two official Beatles singles failed to make either number one or number two in the chart during the 60s. Which two?

7   What was the semolina pilchard doing?

8   Who instigated "Beatle" haircuts?

9   Which Beatles' album featured 'It's Only A Northern Song' and 'It's All Too Much'?

10 Which Beatles' song had the working title of 'Scrambled Egg'?

1   In 1964 Jack Good produced the TV spectacular *Around the Beatles*, John, Paul, George and Ringo played characters from *A Midsummer Night's Dream*. Who played what?

2   British playwright Joe Orton submitted a script to the Beatles as a possible follow-up film to *A Hard Day's Night* and *Help*. What was it called?

3   Who were the Beatmakers?

4   Whose drawing appeared on the cover of the 1967 Beatles fan club record 'Christmastime Is Here Again'?

5   What was the song George Harrison wrote about a box of chocolates?

6   Who was the first Beatle to release a solo LP and what was it called?

7   What pseudonym did Paul McCartney use when producing 'I'm The Urban Spaceman' for the Bonzo Dog Doo-Dah Band?

8   Which Beatles song was about the Maharishi?

9   Which Beatles song was originally going to be called "The Void"?

10 From which group did Ringo join the Beatles?

QUIZ 9	THE BOSS

All the questions in this quiz are about the career and recordings of Bruce Springsteen.

1   What is the name of Springsteen's backing band?

2   What Springsteen song became a hit for the Patti Smith Group?

3   What was Bruce Springsteen's first British Top Ten single?

4   What Springsteen song did Frankie Goes To Hollywood perform on the American television show *Saturday Night Live*?

5   Who took 'Fire' into the British Top 40?

6   On what album does 'In Candy's Room' appear?

7   Who scored a UK Top Forty hit with a cover version of 'Dancing In The Dark'?

8   What New Jersey town did Bruce Springsteen make famous?

9   Of what group is former Springsteen sideman Steve Van Zandt leader?

10 What act took 'Blinded By The Light' to number one in America?

11 Who is Bruce's saxophonist?

12 What 60s star enjoyed a comeback in the early 80s with Bruce's patronage?

13 On what album does 'Jungleland' appear?

14 What Springsteen album was taped on a four-track cassette recorder?

15 On what American number one single has Bruce vocalized?

1   What legendary talent executive signed Springsteen to Columbia Records?

2   Who is Bruce Springsteen's manager?

3   What was Bruce's first American Top Ten single?

4   What Springsteen song responds to the death of Elvis Presley?

5   What famed film-maker directed the 'Dancing In The Dark' video?

6   Who authored the Bruce biography *Born to Run*?

7   By what alternate title did 'Fourth Of July, Asbury Park' become known?

8   What was Bruce Springsteen's biggest UK hit single prior to the release of material from *Born in the U.S.A.*?

9   What concert clip was shown on both *The Old Grey Whistle Test* and *Heroes of Rock and Roll*?

10 At what venue did Bruce Springsteen first perform in London?

11 What Springsteen song was the follow-up to the hit mentioned in section A, question 10?

12 In what film was Bob Seger music substituted for Springsteen's when the motion picture company did not reach a deal with Bruce's record label?

13 What Jimmy Cliff song has Springsteen released?

14 On what album does 'Wreck On The Highway' appear?

15 What Isley Brothers song has Bruce performed in concert?

1 On what album does 'Santa Claus Is Coming To Town' appear?

2 What famed film-maker directed the *Born in the U.S.A.* short?

3 What group recorded the song mentioned in section B, question 7?

4 On what album did Springsteen's Mitch Ryder medley appear?

5 What photographer took the cover snaps for *Born in the U.S.A.*?

6 Who was Bruce's songwriting collaborator in the group the Castiles?

7 What Springsteen song did Alvin Stardust cover?

8 In what publication did Jon Landau's famous line "I saw rock and roll future and its name is Bruce Springsteen" appear?

9 On what single did former Turtles Flo and Eddie sing backing vocals?

10 What Springsteen song mentions James Dean and Burt Reynolds?

11 What Chiffons song was recorded for *Born to Run* but not released?

12 Springsteen's most collectible US single was a Columbia Playback version of 'Blinded By The Light' for DJs only. The other side was by a different artist. Name that act and the track

13 What duet between Bruce and Jackson Browne has been released?

14 Why are some early copies of *Born to Run* worth over $100?

15 'Dancing In The Dark' was originally a Top Ten US title in 1941. Who was the artist on this different song?

<table>
<tr><td>

QUIZ 10

</td><td>

WEATHER FORECAST

</td></tr>
</table>

Name the "damp" hits for:	Now try these "hot" numbers:
1 Bob Dylan in '68	1 Goombay Dance Band in '82
2 Leo Sayer in '78	2 Cliff Richard in '71
3 Aphrodite's Child in '68	3 Osibisa in '70
4 Bobbie Gentry in '70	4 Cream in '68
5 Biddu in '76	5 Elkie Brooks in '77
6 Frankie Laine in '54	6 Nik Kershaw in '84
7 Randy Crawford in '81	7 Traffic in '67
8 Ann Peebles in '74	8 Status Quo in '68
9 Partridge Family in '73	9 Vanity Fayre in '68
10 Temptations in '68	10 Donna Summer in '79

<table>
<tr><td>

QUIZ 11

</td><td>

SPOT THE PIGEON

</td></tr>
</table>

All these questions involve animals of one sort or another. Insects, fish, birds, amphibians, reptiles and mammals, not to mention creepy-crawlies and other invertebrates – all non-human life is here.

1 Which mis-spelt insects took 'She Loves You' to number one?

2 Which insects took 'Prince Charming' to number one?

3 What form of animal life took 'I'm A Believer' to number one?

4 Who hopped up to number eight with 'The Cutter'?

5 Which mammal went on a summer holiday in 1984?

6 Which insects took 'That'll Be The Day' to number one?

7 Which rodents took 'I Don't Like Mondays' to number one?

8 Which birds were wishing they had a photograph of you?

9 Which amphibians stood together with Paul McCartney at Christmas 1984?

10 Who took 'House Of The Rising Sun' to number one?

11 Which animal did Elvis Presley, Red Sovine and Booker Newbury III all sing about?

12 What was the Singing Sheep's only hit?

13 Which animal did Tight Fit, the Tokens and Karl Denver all say was asleep?

14 Which colourful animal did Culture Club sell a million of?
15 Which bird does Prince know what it sounds like when they cry?
16 What did the Tweets sing (dance)?
17 Which affectionate animals did Cure introduce into the Top Ten?
18 Which reptile did Duran Duran unionize?
19 What was Chas and Dave's talkative burrower?
20. On the wings of what did the Everly Brothers fly back into the charts in 1984?

1 Who has had hits about a bird, a crustacean, a mammal and an insect?
2 Which Banshee is a Creature and a Bird?
3 Which mad pachyderm pleaded for affection in 1969?
4 What insect did Danyel Gerard, Val Doonican and Charlie Gracie all chase?
5 Which birds brought Henry Mancini back into the charts in 1984?
6 Who wrote Lulu's hit 'I'm A Tiger'?
7 Who had a dog named Boo?
8 What was the name of Ahab the Arab's camel?
9 Which quick animal did Sweet and Manfred Mann bring into the Top Ten?
10 Which vicious fish inhabit the Zambesi?
11 Who was "too lazy to crow for day"?
12 Who walked her cat named Dog?
13 Who rode on a nameless horse?
14 Which cross between a sheep and a cow hit the Top Ten, courtesy of a band in turbans?
15 What was the name of the Toy Dolls' big pet?
16 What did Patti Page and Lita Rosa want to know the price of?
17 Which dangerous group hit with 'The Zoo' and 'Another Piece Of Meat'?
18 What animals "ain't what it takes to love me"?
19 Shakin' and Cat Stevens both began their chart careers with hits about the same animal. Which one?
20 Which bird did T. Rex ride into the Top Ten?

1 Which animal did Maria Muldaur suggest should be sent to bed?

2 Who wrote 'Simon Smith And His Amazing Dancing Bear'?

3 Who wrote 'Running Bear'?

4 Which animal precedes Chop, Man and Spanner in the charts?

5 Which animals have been white, crazy and swimming in the charts?

6 What is "a little black bug, from Mexico they say"?

7 Paul McCartney has recorded two songs about his dogs. What are they?

8 Johnny is a joker. What else is he?

9 What animal connects a s-s-single bed, a mockingbird and a burning car?

10 Which animal has hit a higher position in the British charts, the crocodile or the alligator?

11 What is the only instrumental insect to hit number one?

12 What animal do the Captain and Tennille, Freddy Cannon and the Everly Brothers share?

13 Which birds hang out in Smokey Joe's Cafe?

14 What animals have been made of straw and diamonds in the charts?

15 What animals "play clean as country water"?

16 Who has Animal Instinct?

17 Who has "gone where the good doggies go"?

18 What flying objects did Jewel Akens and Alma Cogan both sing about?

19 What asked for 'Just One More Night'?

20 What happened after Billy Connolly took his dog to the V.E.T.?

| ENGLAND SWINGS

Not all songs about places have to be about **American places**. Here are 60 toughies about songs or acts that have turned to the geography of the United Kingdom (that's England, Scotland, Wales and Northern Ireland) for inspiration.

Which acts hit with the following?:

1 'Waterloo Sunset'
2 'Streets Of London'
3 'England Swings'
4 'London Calling'
5 'Winchester Cathedral'
6 'Liverpool Lou'
7 'Finchley Central'
8 'Penny Lane'
9 'Jarrow Song'
10 'Scarborough Fair'
11 'Hersham Boys'
12 '(White Man) In Hammersmith Palais'
13 'Baker Street'
14 'Manchester United'
15 'A Scottish Soldier'
16 'English Country Garden'
17 'England We'll Fly The Flag'/ 'This Time (We'll Get It Right)'
18 'Belfast'
19 'A New England'
20 'Mull Of Kintyre'

Now place the original recordings of these:

1 'Windsor Waltz'
2 'Dick-A-Dum-Dum (King's Road)'
3 'Durham Town (The Leavin')'
4 'London Boys'
5 'Last Night In Soho'
6 'English Civil War (Johnny Comes Marching Home)'
7 'The Greatest Cockney Ripoff'
8 'Belfast Boy'
9 'London Town' (either one of two possible correct answers will do)
10 'Victoria'
11 Which two acts with Wigan as part of their names hit the UK Top 20?
12 Who had a hit in 1960 with a song more usually associated with Dame Vera Lynn? The song was about the Kent coastline.
13 The same gentleman's first hit mis-spelled his home county. Name the hit.

14   Who wrote 'A New England', the 1985 hit referred to in section A, question 19?

15   Who exhorted us to 'Do The Strand'?

16   Who had success *Selling England By The Pound*?

17   Whose number one LP in 1981 was entitled *No Sleep Till Hammersmith*?

18   Which band (fairly well known in the mid-seventies) named themselves after a sign that was well known to motorists leaving north London?

19   Where did Fiddler's Dram go?

20   Slade's first chart single for three years was actually an EP that featured their performance at a well-known rock festival. The hit was entitled *Slade Alive At ——— '80* – what English town fills the gap?

1   Who had a minor hit with a song called 'Belfast' in 1985 (not the song that was a top tenner for a well-known act in 1977)?

2   Who had a best-selling album of *Great Songs From Great Britain* in 1962?

3   Who had a best-selling album in the US entitled *McLemore Avenue* in 1970 which featured a deliberate variation on the artwork of the Beatles' *Abbey Road*?

4   Whose 1979 comeback album was called *Broken English*?

5   Who claimed 'Every Man Must Have A Dream'?

6   Who sang about 'Green Street Green'?

7   What was the title of Arsenal FC's musical contribution to 20th Century culture in 1971?

8   Who played the memorable sax solo on Gerry Rafferty's 'Baker Street'?

9   Who broke through with 'Fog On The Tyne'?

10   Who caught the 'Last Train To London'?

11   And who caught the 'Next Plane To London'?

12   What British city was credited on the label of Paul McCartney's live version of 'Coming Up' (which became a number one single in the States)?

13   What British city is mentioned in ABBA's 'Super Trouper'?

14   Who recorded a track called 'The British Opera' on their album *Odessa*?

15   Who hit number one in the US, aged 13, with a platter that never got beyond number 12 in the UK, his home territory?

16 With which famous song about the UK capital did the Anti-Nowhere League enjoy minor UK chart success in 1982?

17 Who recorded 'Viva El Fulham'?

18 Who took Margate into the charts in 1982?

19 Who did the 'British Hustle'?

20 Which great instrumentalist played the 'Britannia Rag' in 1952?

QUIZ 13	SUNGLASSES

Spot the artists behind the shades

1

2

3

4

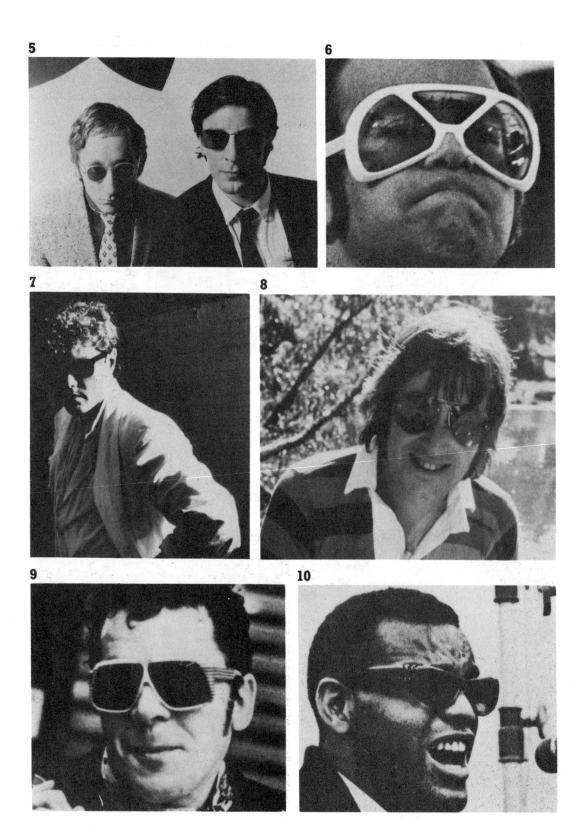

11

12

13

14

THREE STEPS TO HEAVEN

In the three sections below the titles that bear the same numbers are all by the same artists. For example, A1, B1 and C1 are by a single act. Scoring in this quiz is the reverse of most others. If you can guess the artist from the A title, you earn three points. You score two if you require both the A and B clues, and if you identify the artist after all three titles, take one point.

1 'Physical Attraction'
2 'Lalena'
3 'Am I The Same Girl'
4 'L. A. Is My Lady'
5 'Gasoline Alley'
6 'I'm Afraid Of Me'
7 'I'll Get You'
8 'Shattered'
9 'Obscene Phone Caller'
10 'Run Run Run'
11 'Erotic City'
12 'All This Love'
13 'Let Me Be Lonely'
14 'The Fat Man'
15 'Ask The Lonely'
16 'I Truly Truly Believe'
17 'White Feathers'
18 '(Sooner Or Later) One Of Us Must Know'
19 'I Forgot To Remember To Forget'
20 'I Missed Again'
21 'Lady Writer'
22 'Hey Love'
23 'Wandering Stranger'
24 'Johnny Can't Read'
25 'Let Me Tell You Babe'
26 'Tie Your Mother Down'
27 'She Loved Like Diamond'
28 '(Remember Me) I'm The One Who Loves You'
29 'Paper Cup'
30 'He Said The Same Things To Me'

1 'Borderline'
2 'Atlantis'
3 'I Close My Eyes And Count To Ten'
4 'All The Way'
5 'Young Turks'
6 'Miss Me Blind'
7 'Here There And Everywhere'
8 'Have You Seen Your Mother Baby Standing In The Shadow'
9 'Peeping Tom'
10 'Bad Weather'
11 'I Wanna Be Your Lover'
12 'Time Will Reveal'
13 'Don't Make Me Over'
14 'Be My Guest'
15 'Shake Me Wake Me'
16 '(I Know) I'm Losing You'
17 'Hang On Now'
18 'Baby Stop Crying'
19 'Too Much'
20 'If Leaving Me Is Easy'
21 'Tunnel Of Love'
22 'I Don't Know Why'
23 'Truly'
24 'Dirty Laundry'
25 'Nature Boy'
26 'Flash'
27 'Paint Me Down'
28 'Return To Me'
29 'Wedding Bell Blues'
30 'I Can't Stay Mad At You'

1 'Like A Virgin'
2 'Mellow Yellow'
3 'I Only Want To Be With You'
4 'Strangers In The Night'
5 'Maggie May'
6 'Karma Chameleon'
7 'Hey Jude'

8 '(I Can't Get No) Satisfaction'

9 'Somebody's Watching Me'

10 'Baby Love'

11 'Purple Rain'

12 'Rhythm Of The Night'

13 'Walk On By'

14 'Blueberry Hill'

15 'Reach Out I'll Be There'

16 'Just My Imagination (Running Away With Me)'

17 'Too Shy'

18 'Lay Lady Lay'

19 'Hound Dog'

20 'One More Night'

21 'Sultans Of Swing'

22 'I Just Called To Say I Love You'

23 'All Night Long'

24 'The Boys Of Summer'

25 'When I Fall In Love'

26 'Bohemian Rhapsody'

27 'True'

28 'Memories Are Made Of This'

29 'Aquarius/Let The Sunshine In'

30 'End Of The World'

QUIZ 15	HALFWAY TO PARADISE

The following song titles are incomplete. The full title starts either before or after the brackets. Give the full title of the song and name the group or artist who recorded it.

1 (Win Place Or Show)

2 (Down To The Ground)

3 (I Believe In Love)

4 (Have Taken Over The Asylum)

5 (The Telephone Answering Machine Song)

6 (Where My Rosemary Goes)

7 (It's Caught Me In The Spotlight)

8   (With No Big Fat Woman)
9   (But My Love)
10   (Don't Hurt Me)
11   (Evergreen)
12   (Remember The Days Of The)
13   (Give Me Your Heart)
14   (At The Copa)
15   (But In My Heart Its Spring)
16   (I Gave You The Best Years Of My Life)
17   (Go For It)
18   (Take A Look At Me Now)
19   (That's My Home)
20   (All Night)

1   (Three Stars Will Shine Tonight)
2   (Got My Beer In The Sideboard Here)
3   (But My Baby Loves To Dance)
4   (The Best You Can Do)
5   (Life Could Be A Dream)
6   (The First Time)
7   (Give Me Peace On Earth)
8   (In A Rock 'n' Roll Band)
9   (Shake Shake Shake)
10   (Andes Pumpsa Daesi)
11   (Retribution)
12   (Night-clubbing)
13   (Call Me)
14   (Be Heard)
15   (It's Just A Story)
16   (Finger On The Trigger)
17   (The Queen Of The Blues)
18   (Theme from Tubular Bells)
19   (If I Had A Photograph Of You)
20   (Give A Little Bit More)

1   (Johnny Comes Marching Home)
2   (The Human Zoo)
3   (The Savage Seven Theme)
4   (We Used To Know)
5   (Mon Amour)
6   (Le Colline Sono In Fioro)
7   (Man It Was Mean)
8   (Doctor Doctor)
9   (King's Road)
10 (Love On Delivery)
11 (Can't Live Without You)
12 (Tous Les Bateaux, Tous Les Oiseaux)
13 (West Runs South)
14 (Skanga)
15 (Spurs Are On The Way To Wembley)
16 (And The Birds Were Singing)
17 (The Wizard Of Aus)
18 (The Waltz Joan Of Arc)
19 (Muhammad Ali)
20 (Let It Begin With Me)

QUIZ 16	BAD OLD DAYS

Listed below are song titles from the 60s. One word has been omitted from each title. All you have to do is find that one word.

1   'Hubble Bubble . . . . and Trouble' – Manfred Mann
2   'It's Good News . . . .' – Hedgehoppers Anonymous
3   'Rainbow . . . .' – Love Affair
4   'Quick Joey . . . .' – Kasenetz-KatzSinging
                                          Orchestral Circus
5   'Lights Of . . . .' – Scott Walker
6   'Nut . . . .' – B. Bumble and the Stingers
7   'Let There Be . . . .' – Sandy Nelson
8   'Mr . . . . Man' – Byrds
9   'A . . . . Concerto' – Toys
10 'King . . . . In Reverse' – Hollies

1 'The Rise And Fall Of .... Bunt' – Shadows
2 'Holy ....' – Lee Dorsey
3 '.................... In Moscow' – Kenny Ball
4 '.................... Birthday' – Shane Fenton
5 'The Cruel ....' – Dakotas
6 'Message To ....' – Adam Faith
7 'Can You Please .... Out Your Window' – Bob Dylan
8 'Soul and ....' – Righteous Brothers
9 'Lovers Of The World ....' – David and Jonathan
10 'Night Of The .... Grass' – Troggs

1 'Hush Not A Word To ....' – John Rowles
2 'Just A Little Bit ....' – Herman's Hermits
3 'Little Miss ....' – Helen Shapiro
4 'Kissin' ....' – Elvis Presley
5 'The Special ....' – Val Doonican
6 'He's Got No ....' – Searchers
7 'Princess In ....' – Gene Pitney
8 'Lady ....' – Peter and Gordon
9 'A Love Like ....' – Ike and Tina Turner
10 'You've Not ....' – Sandie Shaw

| QUIZ 17 | SATURDAY NIGHT AT THE MOVIES |

All these questions concern rock in the cinema.

Who were the stars of the following movies?

1 *Jailhouse Rock*
2 *The Young Ones*
3 *A Hard Day's Night*
4 *Blue Hawaii*
5 *Ferry Cross The Mersey*
6 *Summer Holiday*
7 *Grease*
8 *Tommy*
9 *Flame*
10 *Tommy The Toreador*

Who performed the title song of:

11 *Where The Boys Are*
12 *Wild In The Country*
13 *Let It Be*
14 *Stayin' Alive*
15 *The Girl Can't Help It*
16 *Because They're Young*
17 *Yellow Submarine*
18 *High School Confidential*
19 *Fame*
20 *Shaft*

Who played the title role in:

1 *The Buddy Holly Story*
2 *The Hank Williams Story*
3 *The Glenn Miller Story*
4 *The Tommy Steele Story*
5 *Lady Sings The Blues*

Who was the star of:

6 *The Fastest Guitar Alive*
7 *Rhythm and Greens*
8 *I've Gotta Horse*
9 *The Duke Wore Jeans*
10 *Catch Us If You Can*

Which film soundtracks contain the following tracks:

11 'The Heat Is On' by Glenn Frey and 'Neutron Dance' by the Pointer Sisters
12 'I Just Called To Say I Love You' by Stevie Wonder and 'Moments Aren't Moments' by Dionne Warwick
13 'Jive Talkin' ' by the Bee Gees and 'A Fifth of Beethoven' by Walter Murphy
14 'Maxwell's Silver Hammer' by Steve Martin and 'Mean Mr. Mustard' by Frankie Howerd
15 'Going Up The Country' by Canned Heat and 'With A Little Help From My Friends' by Joe Cocker

Which film featured the following stars:

16 Craig Douglas and Helen Shapiro
17 Gene Vincent, Little Richard, Fats Domino and Eddie Cochran
18 Elvis Presley, Ann-Margret
19 Chubby Checker, Marcels
20 David Essex, Adam Faith, Larry Hagman

1 Which number one hitmaker directed *Myra Breckinridge*?
2 What was the biggest UK hit single from the film *Footloose*?
3 Which was the first non-Beatle film that Paul McCartney wrote music for?
4 Which was Elvis Presley's final feature film?
5 Name any three films featuring American DJ Alan Freed (one point each)
6 Which film starred Bobby Darin, and included music performed by the Bobby Darin Orchestra?
7 What do the songs 'Alfie', 'The Man Who Shot Liberty Valance' and 'The Ballad Of Bonnie And Clyde' have in common?
8 Who sang on the soundtrack of both *Saturday Night Fever* and *Jesus Christ Superstar*?
9 Which film first made 'Rock Around The Clock' a hit?

10　Which film featured, among others, Fats Domino, Jerry Lee Lewis, Carl Perkins and Charlie Gracie?

11　Which film featured Ray Charles as a gun-store owner?

12　In which film did Cliff Richard sing 'Shrine On The Second Floor'?

13　Which hit vocalist and drummer featured in both *Rebel Without A Cause* and *Rock Pretty Baby*?

14　In which film was 'Born To Be Wild' by Steppenwolf heavily featured?

15　Which feature-length cartoon gave rise to a number one hit single (be careful)

16　Which chart-topping artist played his first non-singing role in 'How I Won The War'?

17　What was the theme tune of the film *Midnight Cowboy*, and who sang it?

18　Who played the part of Danny Fisher, and in what film?

19　Two Sidney Poitier movies have produced US number ones. One was *Blackboard Jungle*, but what was the other one?

20　Which film was loosely based on the life of Janis Joplin, and who played the leading role?

QUIZ 18	DESPERATE BUT NOT SERIOUS

A quiz about records and/or songs that are humorous, in the opinion of their producer, at least. This wide-ranging three-parter also involves the odd novelty or freak hit, whose makers' original intentions might not have been to raise a laugh.

Who achieved immortality with the following? All were UK chart hits.

1　'Come Outside'

2　'You Are Awful'

3　'Save Your Love'

4　'The Ugly Duckling'

5　'Long Haired Lover From Liverpool'

6　' 'Ullo John Got A New Motor?'

7　'The Gay Cavalieros'

8　'Cinderella Rockefella'

9　'Mouldy Old Dough'

10　'No Charge'

11　'Nellie The Elephant'

12　'Do The Conga'

13　'Halfway Down The Stairs'

14　'The Clapping Song'

15　'Nice One Cyril'

16　'Happy Talk'

17　'Snot Rap'

18　'The Lone Ranger'

19　'What Are We Gonna Get 'Er Indoors'

20　'Minuetto Allegretto'

1   What duo had a number 25 hit in 1975 with a less than respectful tribute to Telly Savalas' number one smash of the same year?

2   And who wrote the song that gave Telly his brief moment of recording glory: 'If'?

3   Which non-human act spent more time on the charts than any human did in 1974?

4   Which distinguished band owed much of their chart success (one hit) to the enthusiastic radio support from Terry Wogan, who then covered their hit himself?

5   Who advised us that 'You Gotta Be A Hustler If You Wanna Get On' in 1980?

6   Which writer/performer/producer wrote and produced the Scottish Football Team's 1982 hit 'We Have A Dream'?

7   Which weird (for the time) looking bloke, whose name was also that of a character in Dickens' *Christmas Carol*, burst onto the scene in the late sixties with highly individual versions of 'Tiptoe Through The Tulips' and 'Great Balls Of Fire'?

8   Who gave birth to the Piglets?

9   What was the full title of the hit record by Paul Shane and the Yellowcoats, which was also the signature tune of a very popular TV series about a holiday camp?

10   Who had comedy hits on his own, as half of a duo, and as a member of a group? One of his solo hits was a spoken version of a Beatles number one

11   Name the other half of the duo in question 10

12   Which duo have had a succession of humorous hits, but have enjoyed their greatest chart triumph to date with a straight ballad entitled 'Ain't No Pleasing You'?

13   Who had trouble with a 'Police Officer' in late 1984?

14   Which trio of TV stars had five comedy hits (three double-sided) in a little over 12 months beginning December 1974?

15   Who caused both great offence and great amusement in 1966 by means of a tuneless item entitled 'They're Coming To Take Me Away Ha-Haaa!'?

16   Who scored with a brace of Captain Beaky hits?

17   Who sang the original version of 'Fattie Bum Bum'?

18   Under what name did Nigel Planer revive a 1967 Traffic single in 1984?

19   Which two disc-jockeys had a number four hit under the name Laurie Lingo and the Dipsticks in 1976, with a British version of C. W. McCall's very American hit 'Convoy'?

20   Who sent up whom with 'Eat It'?

1 Who moaned in song about his 'Mother-In-Law'?

2 Who advised Frankie Vaughan that he 'Gotta Have Something In The Bank, Frank'?

3 Who sang with Mike Sarne on his second hit 'Will I What'?

4 Which unusual British duo turned up in the charts with an item entitled 'Fan 'Dabi 'Dozi'?

5 Which British comedian scored his one chart hit with 'Shame And Scandal In The Family'?

6 Which American country singer scored his only UK chart success as a performer under the name Bill Parsons – the record 'All American Boy' telling the tale of a rock and roller being called up to the US army?

7 Who had a number one US hit in 1960 with 'Mr Custer'? (His follow-up, 'Mr Livingstone' made number 73)

8 What TV series gave Michael Medwin, Bernard Bresslaw, Alfie Bass and Leslie Fyson a hit in 1958?

9 Pigmeat Markham and Shorty Long had hits in 1968 with identically-titled records, although their songs differed widely from each other. What was the title of their hits?

10 Which of the following was not a hit for Judge Dread? 'Big Six', 'Big Seven', 'Big Eight', 'Big Nine', 'Big Ten'.

11 Which band told the story of communication problems in space on the 1985 charts?

12 Joe South of 'Games People Play' fame had a hit in the States in '58 with 'The Purple People Eater Meets The Witch Doctor'. Which two acts had the hits earlier that year that inspired South's unforgettable opus?

13 Who kissed with confidence?

14 What was the Chipmunks' only UK hit?

15 Which American vocal group preceded the Barron Knights by three years by hitting the UK charts with a medley of parodies of groups and hits of the day?

16 Who stood six foot six and weighed 245?

17 Who revived the Royal Guardsmen 1966 US hit 'Snoopy Vs. The Red Baron' and reached number four in the UK with it in 1973?

18 Who wore short shorts before Freddie and The Dreamers?

19 Who charted in the US with 'I Need Your Help Barry Manilow'?

20 Which UK club disc-jockey took Santa into the top ten twice?

<table>
<tr><td>QUIZ 19</td><td>THE LETTER</td></tr>
</table>

A star's name might take on new meaning if one letter were omitted. From the clues below you are to guess what a chart artist's name might have been but for that letter. For example, "The Thin White Duke gets enthusiastic" could be a clue for "Avid Bowie", David Bowie without the first D.

1 Phone a Beatle
2 Roxy Music man gets his breakfast fibre
3 Kaja bassist asks for charity
4 George Michael eats pig meat!
5 Reg Dwight goes to public school
6 The friendly Beatle
7 'Invisible' girl celebrates with champagne
8 Miss Adu gets depressed
9 Culture Club man of rock
10 Grossly overweight Spandau Ballet vocalist
11 Send the check to the Generation X front man
12 Tom Bailey buys pre-packed vegetables in metal containers
13 Joe Strummer gets a royalty statement
14 Jon Moss goes to the opera for the first time
15 The happiest Spandau Ballet member
16 I sit astride Duran Duran's Simon
17 Paul and Linda McCartney wear Beatle hairpieces
18 A sick Rolling Stone
19 O'Dowd exclaims politely
20 Yazoo man turns to life of crime

1 Throw out a scratchy copy of 'White Christmas'
2 'Mickey' maker overspices her pasta sauce
3 Call out for the 'Memory' maker
4 Toy boy of a Tijuana Brass leader's wife
5 Culture Club guitarist is amused
6 In The Midnight Hour' originator joins a labour protest
7 An extremely poor performance of 'My Way'
8 Songbird who lives 'Downtown'
9 Philip Bailey is replaced by a pine tree
10 Very strange 'Tears' singer
11 He lives in Denmark 'Because They're Young'

12 John Lennon's most negative group

13 'Puppet On A String' vocalist was a witness

14 Stevie Nicks' mother

15 'Bend Me Shape Me' stars hang out with the boys

16 General Johnson's Shakespeare scholars

17 One of the 'Bye Bye Love' siblings cares

18 'Halfway To Paradise' man cooks with a wok

19 Don't re-hire that 'Deck Of Cards' cover merchant

20 He recorded 'Sweet Caroline' for nothing

1 The Wilson brothers perform the *Well-tempered Clavier*

2 Run a 100-yard dash against the 'True Love' female vocalist

3 Motown mogul makes mayhem movies

4 Ranking Roger stakes a wager

5 'I'm Your Puppet' man appears with jars of fruit preserves

6 Massage 1955's most popular female artist

7 'So Much Love' man overcooks his Hot Cross treat

8 The 'Ramblin' Rose' great was related to everyone

9 Clarinettists of the Mr Bilk variety

10 'Mack The Knife' revivalist swore politely

11 They got over the anger they felt when their US smash 'Der Kommissar' didn't do as well in Britain

12 'Bend It' band contains a man with a facial twitch

13 Mink stoles bought for the ladies of Levi Stubbs and Renaldo Benson

14 Engage the 'Kiddio' balladeer

15 The 'I Believe' man starts a queue for persons with his Christian name

16 The 'Old Rivers' chartmaker needs more moisture

17 He's 'Confessin'' that he's gone grazin'

18 They're having a harvest for the Caribbean world

19 The super freak improvises

20 'What's New Pussycat' warbler tries transcendental meditation

<table>
<tr><td>QUIZ 20</td><td>COMMUNICATION BREAKDOWN</td></tr>
</table>

The answers to these hits are to do with some form of communication. Name the hit for:

1 Tom Robinson in '83
2 Orchestral Manoeuvres in the Dark in '83
3 Elvis Costello in '78
4 Stylistics in '75
5 T. Rex in '72
6 Spandau Ballet in '83
7 Box Tops in '67
8 Electric Light Orchestra in '77
9 Buggles in '79
10 In Deep in '83
11 Kissing The Pink in '83
12 Ray Stevens in '72
13 Carpenters in '75
14 David McCallum in '66
15 Barry Manilow in '82
16 Meri Wilson in '77
17 Orchestral Manoeuvres in the Dark in '80
18 Funboy Three in '82
19 Charlie Dore in '79
20 Selecter in '79

<table>
<tr><td>QUIZ 21</td><td>YOU DON'T HAVE TO BE IN THE ARMY TO FIGHT IN THE WAR</td></tr>
</table>

All these questions are in some way connected with wars, soldiers, armies, fighting and other such martial arts.

1 Who hit with 'Love Is A Battlefield'?
2 Who hit with 'Buffalo Soldier'?
3 Who advised young guns to go for it?
4 Who sang of life in England 'Between The Wars'?
5 Which group hit with 'Are Friends Electric'?
6 Which is the only military band (to the end of 1984) to have hit number one in the UK singles chart?
7 Which record spent 40 weeks on the chart without ever climbing higher than number 19?
8 Who took his 'War Baby' to number six?
9 Whose 'War Song' came into the chart at number three, but never hit the top?
10 Who partnered Clint Eastwood on his 'Last Plane (One Way Ticket)' hit?
11 Who hit with the theme from 'Star Wars'?

12 Roger Whittaker's biggest hit, also a minor hit for Elvis Presley, was about a man leaving for the war. What was it called?

13 Which two number one hitmakers starred in the film *The Dirty Dozen*?

14 Whose 'Pipes Of Peace' hit the very top?

15 Who pointed out that "at Waterloo, Napoleon did surrender"?

16 What was the average age of American soldiers in Vietnam?

17 Which theme from a film set in the Korean war reached number one years after the film was released?

18 Who told us what happens "when two tribes go to war"?

19 Which sergeant had a Lonely Hearts Club Band?

20 Who told everyone about the 'A-Bomb in Wardour Street'?

1 Which captain hit number one with a song from a war musical?

2 Which lieutenant hit number one with a tune about bread?

3 Which major's indecisive hit was covered by Wayne Fontana and the Mindbenders?

4 Who originally recorded 'War' that Frankie Goes To Hollywood revived?

5 Which branch of the services did Petula Clark sing about on her first number one hit?

6 Charlie Drake covered Larry Verne's American number one hit tribute to which general?

7 Whose tribes fought with each other, so their love could never be?

8 Who originally recorded 'Soldier Boy'?

9 From which film did the chart-topper 'Wooden Heart' come?

10 Who had a hit with 'French Foreign Legion'?

11 Under what name did Terry Dactyl hit with 'Stop The Cavalry'?

12 Who recorded the pro-Vietnam War American chart-topper, 'The Ballad Of The Green Berets'?

13 Which two stars battled against each other in the charts with 'The Battle Of New Orleans'?

14 Who had a hit with the theme from *Soldier Blue*?

15 Which aptly-named studio group hit with the First World War song, 'Goodbye-ee'?

16 Which Christmas war record hit the Top Ten twice, eight years apart?

17 And who hit with the theme from the film *The Legion's Last Patrol*?

18 Who made the album *Electric Warrior*?

19 Whose biggest hit has been 'Oliver's Army'?

20 Who had a hit about the plane that dropped the atomic bomb on Hiroshima?

1 Into which service were the Everly Brothers called up?

2 What was Elvis Presley's army number?

3 Who starred in *Idle On Parade*?

4 Whose experiences as a soldier inspired the film's plot?

5 How did the group who hit with 'Easier Said Than Done' get their name?

6 Which 50s number one stated that "a soldier is a soldier and when he's on parade an order is an order and has to be obeyed"?

7 Which sailor featured on Paul McCartney's first American number one?

8 Which song about soldiers returning from the war gave Adam Faith a hit?

9 Which Vera Lynn hit of the Second World War also became a hit for the Righteous Brothers?

10 Who hit the charts in 1970 with 'Vietnam'?

11 Which US chart-topping act was named after an American Civil War battlefield?

12 What was the title of the vocal version of the Louis Armstrong hit, 'The Faithful Hussar'?

13 What was the title of the vocal version of the John Williams hit, 'Theme From The Deer Hunter'?

14 Which film theme gave Wing Commander A. E. Sims O.B.E. his only chart hit?

15 Who recorded the anti-Vietnam war anthem 'I-Feel-Like-I'm-Fixing-To-Die Rag'?

16 Which chart-topping band kicked off their British chart career with 'Machine Gun'?

17 What hit connects Michael Medwin, Alfie Bass, Leslie Fyson and Bernard Bresslaw?

18 In which film was David Bowie a prisoner of war of the Japanese?

19 Which number one hitmaker featured in the film *The Great Escape*?

20 What was Blondie's last UK hit?

<table>
<tr><td>QUIZ 22</td><td># REMEMBER (THE DAYS OF THE OLD SCHOOL YARD)</td></tr>
</table>

Some questions about records, songs or even artists with educational connections. There is no danger that you will be asked to name every member of the St Winifred's School Choir.

1 But what was the name of the St Winifred's School Choir's number one single?

2 Who announced that 'School's Out' in 1972?

3 Who hit with 'The Eton Rifles'?

4 'Girls' School' was the flip side of which 2,000,000 seller?

5 Who revived the Gershwin/Gershwin 1935 standard 'It Ain't Necessarily So' (a song that is in some respects a Scripture lesson) in 1984?

6 Who realized that 'There Are More Questions Than Answers' in 1972?

7 What was the name of the group from the Abbey Hey Junior School who had a 1979 hit with 'The Sparrow'?

8 The Kids From Fame, who acted the parts of students at drama school in the TV series *Fame*, had a number three UK hit in 1982. What was the title of the record?

9 Who began a remarkable career with four US number ones, the second being 'ABC'?

10 Which 14-year-old schoolgirl stormed into the UK singles charts in 1961 with 'Don't Treat Me Like A Child'?

11 Which schoolmaster had a number eight hit in Britain in 1973 with 'Gaye'?

12 Which Birmingham-based five-piece band had their public appearances restricted by law after their 1982 UK number one because the younger members of the group had to put educational considerations first?

13 What was the title of the Pink Floyd's first single hit in the UK for 12½ years, which featured a schoolchildren's choir and lyrics that urged teachers to "leave that kid alone"?

14 Headgirl, who had one hit – the *St Valentine's Day Massacre* EP – were a combination of two chart bands, one male and one female. The girls were Girlschool – who were the chaps?

15 Which Rolling Stones classic contained the line "I'm no schoolboy but I know what I like"?

16 Who sang about Mary of the fourth form?

17 Which rock 'n roll record of unparalleled importance was featured in the movie *Blackboard Jungle*?

18 Who revealed all about the Harper Valley P.T.A. (Parents and Teachers Association)?

19 Which Police track told of a relationship between a young girl student and a teacher?

20 Which schoolboy made the top three in 1985 in the company of Sarah Brightman?

1 Which number one hit was inspired by the Californian schoolgirl who shot many of her fellow pupils in the playground (her bizarre excuse became the title of the song)?

2 Which Chuck Berry hit was subtitled 'Ring Ring Goes The Bell'?

3 Who first sang the schoolroom classic 'Wonderful World'?

4 And what is the first line of that immortal song?

5 Who taught us in 1984 'How To Be A Millionaire'?

6 Who sang lead with the Lower Third?

7 Which major 60s group began their UK chart career with 'Good Morning Little Schoolgirl'?

8 Who took 'Teacher' to number four in 1970?

9 What was the title of both the film and record starring Lulu that gave her a number one US smash in 1967? The movie was about a black schoolteacher.

10 Who was taught how to yodel?

11 Which pop star and subsequent Jack of all trades refused to abandon his Cambridge University degree course in 1965 when his first single was a major international hit?

12 Which 60s group (from Hertfordshire), who were much more successful in America than in their home country, acquired a (possibly justified) reputation for intelligence because between them they had passed a reasonably high number of O Levels?

13 Who had a hit with 'History Of The World (Part 1)' in 1980?

14 Who begged 'Teach Me To Twist'?

15 Who had an instrumental hit entitled 'Lesson One' which was simply a variation on the well-known 'Chopsticks' vamp?

16 Who took Shakespeare's sister (not previously regarded as a major figure in English literary history) into the charts in 1985?

17 On the other hand Henry VIII is a major figure in history. Who had an American number one with 'I'm Henry VIII I Am' in 1965?

18 But the above was not actually about the original Henry VIII. Who had a major album success entitled *The Six Wives of Henry VIII* which was historically accurate?

19 Who sang of 'Me And Julio Down By The Schoolyard'?

20 Who sang 'Teach Your Children'?

1 Who wanted to be Teacher's Pet in 1956?

2 Who sang 'Teacher, Teacher' in 1958?

3 Who had hits with both 'School Is Out' and 'School Is In' in America in 1961?

4 Who complained that "Johnny kissed the teacher, he tiptoed up to reach her"?

5 And what was Johnny described as in the same 50s hit?

6 The flip of Cliff Richard's 'I Love You' featured Cliff complaining that his woman was not doing very well in a certain subject. What was the title of the song?

7 Who charted 'Learning The Game'?

8 Another about a Cliff flip. His first record originally featured 'Schoolboy Crush' as the A side, not 'Move it'. Who sang the US original of 'Schoolboy Crush'?

9 Whose first US hit was 'The Class'?

10 Who sang of a 'Swinging School'?

11 Who was 'Stayin' In' because he "punched a buddy in the nose after lunch – now I'm in trouble 'cos the Dean saw the punch"?

12 Which UK number one hit (apart from their own) featured the voices of the St Winifred's School Choir?

13 Who had a 'Vacation' in 1962?

14 Who was "sittin' in class tryin' to read my book" when her baby gave her that special look – and what was the record that told us about this situation?

15 Who compiled the *Dictionary of Soul*?

16 Who had a number one on one side of the Atlantic and a number two on the other with 'Learnin' The Blues'?

17 Who wrote 'Multiplication'?

18 Which song included the refrain "When will they ever learn"?

19 Which film featured its star singing a tribute to his Alma Mater, 'Steadfast, Loyal and True'?

20 Which English act gave chart lessons in love?

UPTOWN FESTIVAL

The following clues all refer to song titles that contain the names of Motown stars. Almost all the famous personalities are recording artists, but a few esteemed songwriters and producers are included in the harder questions. For example, the answer to the clue "Robert Palmer paired Bristol and Wells" would be "Johnny and Mary", Palmer's 1980 hit. The printed answers in the back pages will list the titles we seek and the artists to whom they might be a tribute.

1 Paul Anka loved Miss Ross
2 Culture Club spotted one of Smokey Robinson's group
3 The Poppy Family queried Preston's sense of direction
4 The Undertones chanted the name of a Ruffin brother
5 Nancy and Lee liked Jermaine
6 Gene Pitney vowed to become the "Money" man
7 The Everly Brothers serenaded the only female Miracle
8 The Highwaymen named the Jackson Five's lead singer
9 Adam Faith sent a telegram to the Vandellas' leader
10 Heaven 17 singled out Eddie Kendricks
11 Debbie Reynolds' favourite Marvin Gaye partner
12 Terry Jacks liked 'The Night' boys in the daytime
13 The Rezillos noticed one of the 'Bernadette' group had become a father
14 Paper Lace advised 'Love Machine' vocalist Griffin
15 Clifford T. Ward mentioned Marvin
16 Marilyn McCoo and Billy Davis Jr told Charles Hatcher he needn't have changed his name
17 The Smiths shrug off Smokey Robinson's congratulations
18 Wings noticed a Supreme's unusual pet
19 10 C.C. identified with the 'Gotta See Jane' singer
20 Colin Blunstone denied the 'Shop Around' crew

1　The Beatles loved Miss Reeves
2　Ace wondered in which way Shorty had done it
3　A paranoid robot remembered 'Can I Get A Witness'
4　The Boomtown Rats told of the 'My Guy' girl's schooling
5　Dean Martin went to Thelma
6　Tom Robinson related to the civil rights leader
7　Jefferson Starship liked 'The Tracks Of My Tears'
8　The Bachelors knew Diana Ross' real name
9　Shakin' Stevens couldn't stop saying Teena's name
10　Joan Armatrading singled out David Ruffin
11　Dion and the Belmonts couldn't conceive Stevie's motivation
12　Carole King thought the *Chameleon* crowd sugary
13　Sue Thompson needed Rick for household chores
14　The Dovells noted the 'Someday We'll Be Together' producer stamping his foot
15　Mathis wondered what Wells would whisper
16　Eddie Cochran suggested walking over Mr Long
17　The Four Seasons prayed for a Miracle
18　The Beach Boys paid tribute to a Supreme producer
19　Carol Deene preferred the producer of 'War'
20　Simon and Garfunkel called Claudette

1　The Cupids loved Miss Holloway
2　Bobby Vee didn't want to know about Miss Randolph
3　Elvis Presley wanted more Tatas
4　Tony Sheridan needed a Pointer
5　Susan Maughan eyed the leader of the 'Does Your Mama Know About Me' band
6　Brick paid tribute to the 'Let It All Blow' boys
7　The Who immortalized a Vancouver
8　Craig Douglas noted the weight loss of the artist who coupled 'What The World Needs Now Is Love/Abraham Martin And John'
9　The Beatles thought Wonder's wife beautiful when she issued her first single
10　Perry Como singled out Otis Williams
11　The Corsairs went to Robinson's hang-outs
12　The Teen Queens fell for the originator of 'Leaving Here'
13　Annette looked up to Temptation

14   The Rolling Stones met Hattie's family one at a time
15   The Village Stompers thought Mister Magic unhip
16   John Lennon demanded the 'Smiling Faces Sometimes' singers
17   Maria Muldaur discounted the bulk of the Rare Earth artist
18   Dickie Valentine thought he might be Mr 'Fingertips'
19   David Bowie rationalized his behaviour to Mabel
20   Joey Powers preferred two lovers at twelve o'clock

| QUIZ 24 | A SOLID BOND IN YOUR HEART |

All these questions have something to do with James Bond.

1   Desmond Dekker's first hit?
2   He vocally despatched amorous feelings from behind the iron curtain in 1963
3   James Bond's boss had two hits in 1979; what were they?
4   Which Bond drummed with the Troggs?
5   Which Bond covered the Beatles' 'Ob-La-Di Ob-La-Da' on the Island label in 1968?
6   Which R & B organist died under the wheels of a London underground train?
7   Which 1966 song on the Atlantic label contained the James Bond titles *Dr. No*, *Thunderball*, *Goldfinger*, *Casino Royale* and *From Russia With Love*?
8   Which James Bond theme was released on 21 November 1969 by John Barry?
9   Who had a hit with 'Casino Royale' in 1967?
10   Who sang the theme to *Thunderball* in 1966?

FAME

Many hit songs have been about real people, even if they haven't all been tributes. How many do you remember?

1 Which film star did Madness take to number 11?
2 Who did Scritti Politti pray like?
3 Who did Alvin Stardust feel like?
4 Who did Bananarama say was waiting, talking Italian?
5 Who did Special AKA want to free?
6 Who was Johnny Wakelin's Black Superman?
7 Buddy Holly hit number four with a song about, and written by, a man who never even hit the UK Top 30. Who?
8 Which tribute to Marvin Gaye and Jackie Wilson reached number three early in 1985?
9 Which tribute to Marvin Gaye hit the US Top Ten at the same time?
10 Phil Lynott's 'King's Call' was a tribute to which singer?
11 Which French king did Bow Wow Wow sing about?
12 To whom was Starsound's fourth medley hit a tribute?
13 Who did Chuck Berry ask to roll over?
14 Which comedy duo, who later had a posthumous number two hit of their own, did the Equals sing about in 1968?
15 With whose music (by Ravel) did Richard Hartley and the Michael Reed Orchestra skate into the Top Ten?
16 Whose version of 'God Save The Queen' reached number two?
17 Who was 'Sir Duke' of Stevie Wonder's 1977 number two hit?
18 Whose rap was Mel Brooks' 'To Be Or Not To Be'?
19 Who was the 'Vincent' of Don McLean's number one?
20 Who did Snoopy fight in the two Royal Guardsmen hits?

1 Whose sister did the Smiths escort into the charts in the spring of 1985?

2 Whose last scratch featured in a Barron Knights hit?

3 Clannad and Dick James both had hits, 28 years apart, about the same man. Who?

4 Whose Tartan Army was going to win the 1978 World Cup?

5 Who did we all follow into the Top Ten in May 1985?

6 About whom was 'Claudette' written?

7 Landscape's first hit was about a scientist. Who?

8 Which football team cup squad scored with 'I'm Forever Blowing Bubbles'?

9 Who were the Hollies in reverse?

10 Bob Dylan's 'Knocking On Heaven's Door' was from a film about which two real-life cowboys?

11 Who originally recorded 'I Hear You Knocking', and got a name-check in Dave Edmunds' number one version?

12 Boney M said he was "Russia's greatest love machine". Who?

13 Boney M also sang about a famous American gangster lady. Who?

14 What did Ian Dury say Elvis and Scottie, Wee Willie Harris and some of Buddy Holly were?

15 Which American President had a name-check in Dream Academy's 'Life In A Northern Town'?

16 Bad Manners' follow-up to 'My Girl Lollipop' featured which Biblical pair?

17 Whose funeral did David Essex describe as 'Oh What A Circus'?

18 Which naked medieval horsewoman did Peter and Gordon sing about?

19 Who was Orchestral Manoeuvres in the Dark's 'Maid Of Orleans'?

20 What was Joe diMaggio's nickname, as mentioned by Simon and Garfunkel in 'Mrs Robinson'?

1. Who was Peter Sellers imitating in his recording of 'A Hard Day's Night'?

2. Peter Gabriel's fourth solo hit was about a South African student leader. Who?

3. George Harrison's *All Things Must Pass* triple album included a track called 'It's Johnny's Birthday'. Who was Johnny, and therefore on which day was it recorded?

4. Which singer, jazz guitarist and composer of Tony Bennett's hit, 'The Good Life' has a name-check in Peter Sarstedt's 'Where Do You Go To My Lovely'?

5. Who did John Lennon claim had given him the title for 'Lucy In The Sky With Diamonds'?

6. Who was the 'Man Of Mystery' whose theme the Shadows played?

7. Ozzy Osbourne's second hit concerned which Satanist?

8. Mantovani's number one 'Moulin Rouge' was the theme of a biopic of which artist?

9. Which tennis player sang back-up vocals on Elton John's hit about her team?

10. Which hit song of 1969, recently rerecorded by Culture Club, mentions "Mick and Lady Faithfull"?

11. Who were Spandau Ballet listening to all night long, if what they sang was 'True'?

12. Who owned the farm land on which the Woodstock Festival was held, as mentioned in Joni Mitchell's song?

13. About whom was 'Killing Me Softly With His Song' supposed to have been written?

14. Who "hocked her jewels in 1492", which Jimmy Jones said was 'Good Timin'?

15. Which Top Ten hit of the early 60s included the line, "Cathy's Clown has Don and Phil like they feel that they wanna die"?

16. Who did Bob Dylan dream he saw, according to the *John Wesley Harding* LP?

17. In 'Creeque Alley', who was "getting kinda itchy, just to leave the folk music behind"?

18. Who, according to 'Little Green Apples', is there no such thing as, along with Disneyland, Mother Goose and nursery rhymes?

19. On which Slade hit do they give themselves a name-check?

20. In 'Telegram Sam', Marc Bolan sings that "Bobby's all right". Who is Bobby?

A PICTURE OF YOU

1. He went to America as an actor, made it big as a singer whose group topped the British charts with their first hit – who is he?
2. Of which John Lennon hit single is this the cover?
3. Bristol born Russ Conway topped the charts twice and collected a D.S.M. during the Second World War. What is his real name?
4. Roy Orbison topped the British charts three times with which songs?
5. For which hit group did her brother play drums?
6. The Tornados were originally whose backing group?

7

8

9

10

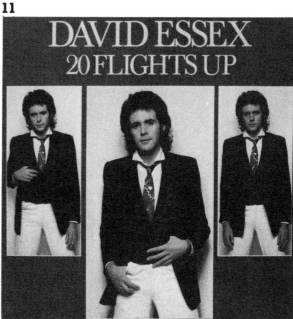
11

DAVID ESSEX
20 FLIGHTS UP

12

The New Christy Minstrels
Three Wheels on my Wagon
Chim Chim Cheree
Last Farewell • Kisses sweeter than wine

7 Who is this "one-hit" chart artist?

8 Jerry Lee Lewis only topped the British charts once – with which song?

9 From which English town do these chaps come?

10 Who is this?

11 What is his real name?

12 The man in the centre of the minstrels had a Top Ten hit in Britain as a soloist in 1965. What was it and who is he?

13 What nationality is Harpo?

14 Who is the chap in the top left-hand corner and what is his link with Jonathan King and ABBA?

15 What is his real name?

16 Who originally recorded 'Run Rudolph Run'?

17 Can you name the line-up?

18 Who are these?

13

HARPO
TELEVISION

14

Um! Um! Um! Um! Um! Um!

fontana

WAYNE FONTANA
and the MINDBENDERS

15

Elvis Costello: Alison: Welcome To The Working Week

16

KEITH RICHARDS
Run Rudolph Run

17

the stranglers

GRIP-LONDON LADY

18

19

19 Who is the guitarist in the shades?

20 What was Bruce Foxton's only Top 40 hit since the Jam split up?

21 Who is the chap with his hands in his pockets (second left) and what is he doing now?

22 What was Eddie Cochran's only British number one?

23 British rocker Vince was never successful here but became a star in which other country?

24 What was Spanky's surname? (Note record company misprint)

25 British born Ian never charted here but had a Top Ten hit in the States in the mid 60s with what record?

26 The six tracks on this EP were recorded in front of a live audience on 9th and 10th February 1959 at which famous London studio?

20

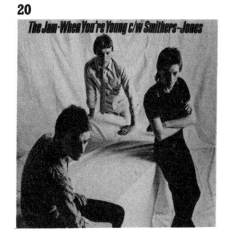

21 **22** **23**

24 **25** **26**

27 Name the man in the pot?

28 What was this lady's biggest British hit?

29 Who is this loving couple?

30 These nine Frenchmen had a British hit with 'The Three
    Bells' in 1959. Who were they?

31 Who is he?

32 He had a Top Ten British hit in 1968, what was it and who is
    he?

33 Who wrote Ricky's big hit 'Hello Mary Lou'?

34 From which Springsteen single is this cover the sleeve?

35 Modern Jazzman Dave Brubeck had three British hits. Can
    you name them?

27

28

29

30

(SONG SUCCESSES IN ENGLISH)

31

32

33

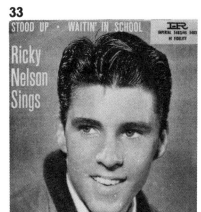

34

35

WE ARE THE WORLD

Social conscience time – 60 questions about hits and artists with a message.

1   Who wrote 'Do They Know It's Christmas?' with Bob Geldof?
2   Who prophesied that 'A Hard Rain's Gonna Fall' in 1973?
3. And who wrote 'A Hard Rain's Gonna Fall' in 1963?
4   Who imagined a world with "no religion, too"?
5   Where has Charlene never been?
6   Who sang about a 'Ghost Town' in 1981?
7   Which Christmas song was a number one for Harry Belafonte in 1957 and for Boney M 11 years later?
8   Who sang about merciful Jesus and took Latin into the charts in 1985?
9   What was the collective name for the aggregation of American stars who recorded 'We Are The World'?
10 And who wrote 'We Are The World'?
11 Who said in 1984 that both war and people were stupid?
12 Which two superstars suggested that black and white people should be in perfect harmony, just like the black and white keys on a piano?
13 Who said we needed "a great big Melting Pot" in 1969?
14 Which famous protest song was Bob Dylan's first UK single hit in 1965?
15 Who claimed we were on the 'Eve Of Destruction' in 1965?
16 Who was George Harrison sweet on in 1971?
17 Which international hit was recorded in a Toronto hotel room?
18 Which group of singers warbled 'O Happy Day'?
19 Who was 'Glad To Be Gay'?
20 Who urged 'White Lines (Don't Do It)' in 1983 and 1984?

1 Who had a dream in 1979 and reached number two with it?

2 Who wrote 'With God On Our Side'?

3 And who covered 'With God On Our Side' on a 1965 EP entitled *The One In The Middle*?

4 Who did Stevie Wonder wish 'Happy Birthday' to in 1981?

5 Who sang 'Give Ireland Back To The Irish' in 1972 and got banned by the BBC?

6 Famed political activist Joan Baez had her biggest UK single hit with a non-message song in 1971. Name it.

7 And what was Joan's only Top Ten UK hit with social comment?

8 Who were 'Part Of The Union'?

9 Who sang about 'Maggie's Farm' 10 years before Mrs Thatcher became leader of the conservative party?

10 And who had a hit with 'Maggie's Farm' the year after she became Prime Minister?

11 Which highly respected American soul singer is now a Reverend and records nothing but gospel songs?

12 Who recorded 'It's Good News Week' in 1965?

13 And who wrote and produced the above smash?

14 Who had hits with 'If I Can Dream' and 'Clean Up Your Own Back Yard' in 1969?

15 What cause have Bronski Beat promoted strongly through their words and music?

16 Who revealed all about 'The Dedicated Follower Of Fashion' in 1966?

17 What did the O'Jays urge us to get onto in 1973?

18 Who (rather optimistically) announced that 'Everything Is Beautiful' in 1970?

19 Which non-motorist exhorted drivers to remain sober via a minor 1984 hit?

20 Who had a number one smash in 1969 with a ballad that told the tale of a poor girl from Naples who found wealth and success but not happiness?

1 Who sang enthusiastically about being 'Young, Gifted and Black' in 1970?

2 What situation was Kenny Rogers in when he begged Ruby not to take her love to town?

3 Why was Rod's Georgie killed?

4 What was the name of the Salvation Army Band that had two chart hits in 1964?

5 Who came up with the unlikely premise that 'There Will Never Be Any Peace (Until God Is Seated At The Conference Table)'?

6 Who originally cried in the chapel?

7 Without whom would Caesar have stood alone according to Buffy St Marie and to Donovan?

8 Who recorded a rush-released single of two Rolling Stones songs in 1967 as a protest against the jail sentences handed out to Keith Richards and Mick Jagger?

9 Where did Whitesnake deny the existence of love in 1980?

10 Who sang about Celia Of The Seals in 1970?

11 Which former engineer of Beatles recordings had a number two smash in the UK with a song he sang and wrote about wild life conservation?

12 Who had a medium-sized hit single in the States entitled 'Ohio' in 1970, inspired by the shooting of students at Kent State University?

13 Who first dealt a 'Deck Of Cards' into the charts?

14 Who put 'King Heroin' into the US charts?

15 Which country singer wrote Roy Orbison's Christmas '64 hit about a poor street vendor, 'Pretty Paper'?

16 Who combined 'Silent Night' with a news bulletin to great effect in 1966?

17 Who followed up a big anti-war song with 'Stop The War Now' in 1971?

18 Who made number four in the UK charts in 1970 with a revival of a Newcastle-based group's 1964 number one that warned of the perils of gambling?

19 Who had a hit in 1977 that was inspired by the Berlin Wall?

20 Who wrote the Byrds' second US number one 'Turn, Turn, Turn'?

<table>
<tr><td>QUIZ 28</td><td>BE STIFF</td></tr>
</table>

QUIZ 28

BE STIFF

This quiz concerns the British independent label Stiff Records: its artists, its hits, its turkeys.

1 According to his Top 20 hit, where was Jona Lewie always found at parties?

2 The Blockheads appeared on what number one?

3 What was Elvis Costello's first chart single?

4 Who made a hit of Billy Bragg's 'A New England'?

5 Who had a Top 40 cover of Carla Thomas' 'B-A-B-Y'?

6 Who recorded the anthem 'Sex 'n' Drugs 'n' Rock 'n' Roll'?

7 What was Madness' number one?

8 What was Tracey Ullman's highest charting single?

9 Who partnered Dave Stewart on the number one 'It's My Party'?

10 Alvin Stardust returned to the Top Ten after a seven-year absence with what Stiff release?

11 Who brandished the 'Swords Of A Thousand Men'?

12 Ian Dury and the Blockheads stayed on the album charts an impressive ninety weeks with what LP?

13 Who recorded the original version of Tracey Ullman's 'My Guy' and under what title?

14 What was Jona Lewie's 1980 Top Three Christmas hits?

15 What Ian Dury hit was subtitled 'Part 3'?

16 What was Elvis Costello's first album?

17 What punk group paid tribute to 'New Rose'?

18 Lene Lovich reached the Top Three with what single?

19 What Elvis Costello A-side was later covered by Linda Ronstadt?

20 Alvin Stardust's 'A Wonderful Time Up There' was a revival of whose 1958 number two?

1 Who had the first single released on Stiff?
2 Who were the "One Chord Wonders"?
3 Who partnered Dave Stewart on 'What Becomes Of The Brokenhearted'?
4 On what EP did 'Night Boat To Cairo' appear?
5 What former Brinsley Schwarz member had an American hit on Stiff called 'Hold On'?
6 What was Elvis Costello's first Stiff single?
7 On what single did Ian Dury opine he could have worked at Fulham Broadway station?
8 Whose EP *Snuff Rock* was based on their live show?
9 Who travelled the 'Whole Wide World'?
10 Before he joined Stiff Jona Lewie reached the top three with a dinosaur band. What was it?
11 What Motorhead hit was originally recorded for release on Stiff?
12 Name three Belle Stars?
13 What was the first Madness single on Stiff?
14 What Lene Lovich hit was co-written by Thomas Dolby?
15 On what single was the question "Are we not men?" answered "We are Devo!"?
16 Madness topped the album chart in what year?
17 Who recorded 'I Think We're Alone Now' in Japanese?
18 What West End original cast album appeared on Stiff?
19 What LP was Stiff's tribute to the American President?
20 What act with Stiff in its name never appeared on Stiff?

1 What male artist covered Sandy Posey's 'Born A Woman'?
2 What Stiff release was subtitled 'Mein Schmerz'?
3 What group had the live album serial prefix Trubz?
4 Who fronted The Crowns?
5 The Blockheads' saxophonist released an unsuccessful solo 45, 'Saxophone Man'. Who was he?
6 What were Ten Pole Tudor doing with their baby?
7 'Caravan Man' was one of Stiff's first 10 issues. Who was the artist?
8 Who led the Psychedelic Rowdies?
9 Who released a double B-side that included 'Texas Chainsaw Massacre Boogie'?

10 Devo appeared on what label distributed by Stiff?

11 Name one of several artists who released their own cover versions of 'Be Stiff'

12 What was unusual about the photo of the Damned on the back cover of early copies of *Damned Damned Damned*?

13 Who led the Voidoids?

14 Who sent out 'Semaphore Signals'?

15 What Welsh rocker appeared on Stiff with a cover of Chuck Berry's 'Jo Jo Gunne'?

16 Who led the Deviants?

17 Who was billed with the backing group the Cable Layers?

18 Who was the artist on the second Stiff single, 'Between The Lines'?

19 Graham Parker's backing group released Stiff singles. Name the group.

20 The backing musicians on Elvis Costello's first LP evolved into what extremely successful American band?

| QUIZ 29 | BACK TO THE SIXTIES |

This is the second probe about a specific year. Already (if you're going through the book from front to back) you've been challenged about 1959. This one is entirely about 1965.

Who had these 1965 biggies?:

1 'The Game Of Love'
2 'True Love Ways'
3 '(I Can't Get No) Satisfaction'
4 'Help!'
5 'Heart Full Of Soul'
6 'My Generation'
7 'Almost There'
8 'Here Comes The Night'
9 'Yeh Yeh'
10 'Concrete and Clay'

11 'Tired Of Waiting For You'
12 'I Got You Babe'
13 'Tears'
14 'Make It Easy On Yourself'
15 'I'm Alive'
16 'Crying In The Chapel'
17 'The Price Of Love'
18 'Mr Tambourine Man'
19 'King Of The Road'
20 'The Minute You're Gone'

Who had these 1965 not-so-biggies?:

1	'Oh No Not My Baby'	11	'When I Get Home'
2	'Baby I'm Yours'	12	'Take Me For What I'm Worth'
3	'On My Word'	13	'Mary Anne'
4	'The Time In Between'	14	'You Make It Move'
5	'Do The Clam'	15	'It's The Same Old Song'
6	'I Hear A Symphony'	16	'Just A Little Bit Better'
7	'Honey I Need'	17	'Something Better Beginning'
8	'Everybody Knows'	18	'That's Why I'm Crying'
9	'With These Hands'	19	'Everybody's Gonna Be Happy'
10	'He's Got No Love'	20	'It's Growing'

1 Who were Chris, Frank, John and Mike?

2 Whom did Marianne Faithfull beat in the chart stakes with 'This Little Bird'?

3 Which hit album of the year contained the track 'Act Naturally?'

4 Which album, partly recorded in 1965, was not issued in the UK until 1977, when it shot to the top of the charts?

5 'Eve Of Destruction', 'Hang On Sloopy' and 'Yesterday' were three consecutive US number ones in 1965. What strange coincidence linked these hits?

6 Which US group, which enjoyed virtually no success in the UK in 1965, began their recording career in January that year with the first of seven consecutive Top Ten hits in America, the last of which was 'Green Grass' in 1966?

7 Who were Caesar and Cleo and how did they miss out on a hit?

8 Who sang the 'Ballad Of Cat Ballou' in the Lee Marvin movie *Cat Ballou*?

9 Who sang the James Bond song of '65 and what was both it and the movie called?

10 Who answered 'Eve Of Destruction' with 'The Dawn Of Correction'?

11 Which two acts urged us to 'Do The Freddie'?

12 Which US city provided Dean Martin with a US hit?

13 Which three acts were the only ones to top the UK album charts in 1965, along with the soundtrack of 'The Sound Of Music'?

14   Who is Lynn Ripley?

15   Which protest song writer had a minor UK hit with 'Sins Of The Family'?

16   Who covered the Lennon/McCartney song 'You've Got To Hide Your Love Away' with fair singles success?

17   Who won the Eurovision song contest in 1965? Name country, artist and song.

18   And what was the UK entry? Name artist and song.

19   Who covered the Bob Dylan song 'It's All Over Now Baby Blue' with fair singles success?

20   Who served a writ on the Byrds as soon as they stepped off the plane from the States to begin their first UK visit?

There are connections between all sorts of unlikely people in the record and charts world, for all sorts of unlikely reasons. This quiz asks you to find out the connections between people and records which might not at first appear to be connected.

In Section A, we ask you to put the titles of hit singles into the blanks, so that the whole paragraph makes sense. In Section B, we ask you to find the connection between various people, a connection that might be very obscure or blindingly obvious.

...... was a hit title for Eden Kane, and also for Stevie Wonder. The flip of the Stevie Wonder record, ..., was an even bigger hit, but not his biggest. That was ...... which won an Oscar, as did ......, Frank Sinatra's first chart-topper in Britain. Sinatra's long-lasting record-breaking single ...... had English lyrics by Paul Anka, who wrote his own number one, ..., as well as Buddy Holly's, ... Holly sang lead on one other chart-topper, ... by the Crickets, whose first hit without Holly was ......, which Holly also recorded separately. The Crickets' final chart hit in Britain was ......, ironically a song written by Ritchie Valens, who died with Buddy Holly. Valens' only hit in Britain, ..., was covered by Marty Wilde, while another of his songs, ..., was a hit for Tommy Steele. Steele hit with two covers of Guy Mitchell songs, the first of which, ..., was a number one hit for both artists. This chart feat was also achieved by ......, as recorded by Perez Prado and Eddie Calvert, and also by ......, which was a number one for Rosemary Clooney and 26 years later for Shakin' Stevens. Shaky also took Frankie Vaughan's number two hit of 1956, ..., to the top 25 years later, and, changing colours, took his version of ...... nine places higher than Elvis had managed 18 years before. One of Elvis' most recent hits has been his version of ......, a song written and originally charted by Billy Swan, who also took Elvis' classic ...... into the charts three years before Presley hit the British charts with this song. The only single that Elvis ever has a writing credit on was ......, which has also been a hit for such diverse acts as Richard Chamberlain and Roland Rat.

What is the connection between the following:

1   Philip Bailey and Phil Collins
2   Phil Collins and Supremes
3   Supremes and Cliff Richard
4   Cliff Richard and Olivia Newton-John
5   Olivia Newton-John and Kenneth McKellar
6   Kenneth McKellar and Engelbert Humperdinck
7   Engelbert Humperdinck and Siouxsie and the Banshees
8   Siouxsie and the Banshees and Creatures
9   Creatures and Tears For Fears
10   Tears For Fears and King Kurt
11   King Kurt and Bobby Darin
12   Bobby Darin and Buddy Holly
13   Buddy Holly and Bo Diddley
14   Bo Diddley and Pretty Things
15   Pretty Things and Gladys Knight
16   Gladys Knight and Stevie Wonder
17   Stevie Wonder and Bob Marley
18   Bob Marley and Eric Clapton
19   Eric Clapton and Jack Bruce
20   Jack Bruce and Manfred Mann
21   Manfred Mann and Mike d'Abo
22   Mike d'Abo and Gary Glitter
23   Gary Glitter and Murray Head
24   Murray Head and Björn Ulvaeus
25   Björn Ulvaeus and ABBA
26   ABBA and Blancmange
27   Blancmange and Searchers
28   Searchers and Frankie Goes To Hollywood
29   Frankie Goes To Hollywood and Gerry and the Pacemakers
30   Gerry and the Pacemakers and Captain Sensible
31   Captain Sensible and Damned
32   Damned and Public Image Limited
33   Public Image Limited and Sex Pistols
34   Sex Pistols and Bow Wow Wow
35   Bow Wow Wow and Culture Club
36   Culture Club and Band Aid

37 Band Aid and USA for Africa
38 USA for Africa and Michael Jackson
39 Michael Jackson and Paul McCartney
40 Paul McCartney and Beatles
41 Beatles and Earth Wind and Fire
42 Earth Wind and Fire and Philip Bailey

which brings us back to where we started

QUIZ 31	NOTHING RHYMED

Here's 60 questions about instrumentals. In these days of extended mega-mixes it's rare for a hit to be without words somewhere in the 12 inches, but there are still a few smashes that more or less dispense with the larynx. See what you can recall about the wordless ones.

Who recorded the first instrumental chart version of these titles?

1   'Kon-Tiki'
2   'Because They're Young'
3   'Wheels'
4   'Flying'
5   'Blue Peter'
6   'Magic Fly'
7   'The Rise And Fall Of Flingel Bunt'
8   'Pepper Box'
9   'Oxygene Part IV'
10 'Rodrigo's Guitar Concerto De Aranjuez'
11 'Stranger On The Shore'
12 'March Of The Siamese Children'
13 'Scarlett O'Hara'
14 'Groovin' With Mr Bloe'
15 'Roulette'
16 'Theme from "A Summer Place"'
17 'Theme from "Shaft"'
18 'Clog Dance'
19 'Amazing Grace'
20 'Walking In Rhythm'

And who scored home runs with these (some only in the American charts)?

1. 'On The Rebound'
2. 'Kommotion'
3. 'Hocus Pocus'
4. 'Trudie'
5. 'Last Date'
6. 'Maroc 7'
7. 'Robot'
8. 'Let's Have A Ding Dong'
9. 'Autumn Leaves'
10. 'Theme from "Summer Of 42"'
11. 'China Tea'
12. 'Rise'
13. 'Pick Up The Pieces'
14. 'America'
15. 'Hang 'Em High'
16. 'Cast Your Fate To The Wind'
17. 'Il Silenzio'
18. 'Teen Beat'
19. 'Honky Tonk'
20. 'Ballad Of Paladin'

1. Who conducted the Love Unlimited Orchestra?
2. Which West Coast instrumental surf group had US hits with 'Out of Limits' and 'Batman Theme'?
3. What connection does Mike Oldfield have with Fratton Park?
4. Which Cuban-born band leader had an international hit in 1958 with the instrumental 'Patricia'?
5. Which jazz–rock band had a hit on the short-lived Infinity label in 1979 with 'Morning Dance'?
6. Duane Eddy's first major hit was 'Rebel Rouser' in 1958. Who recorded 'The Son Of Rebel Rouser' in 1964?
7. Which major US male vocalist had one instrumental hit credited to his orchestra entitled 'Come September' in the middle of a run of vocal hits that stretched from 1958 to 1966?
8. Which of these acts was an instrumental one as far as the US and UK hit parades were concerned: The Chantays. The Chantels, Chanson?
9. And what was the big 1963 hit of the answer to question 8?
10. Who had a fifth of Beethoven?
11. Who did Whistling Jack Smith claim he had been?
12. What major recording artist did the composer of 'Wheels' produce?
13. What was the title of the album by Andrew Lloyd Webber that featured his brother Julian on 'cello and was based on the theme from Paganini's *A Minor Caprice for Violin*?

14 And who had a single smash in the UK in 1954 with 'Rachmaninoff's 18th Variation On A Theme By Paganini'?

15 Which instrumental act has had most British number ones, and how many?

16 Which keyboard wizard had hit albums with *Criminal Record* and *1984*?

17 Who came from Summer Set?

18 Who recorded 'The Hustle' with 'the Soul City Symphony'?

19 Who wrote and produced the Tornados' 'Telstar' in 1962?

20 Which Mersey combo scored with 'The Cruel Sea'?

QUIZ 32	HERE IS THE NEWS

All these acts had hit singles with the word 'new' or 'news' in the title. Name the hit for:

1 T. Rex in '75

2 Vapors in '80

3 Jam in '78, '80

4 Rush in '82

5 Depeche Mode in '81

6 Melanie in '72

7 Stylistics in '74

8 Gillan in '81

9 Bee Gees in '67

10 Eagles in '77

11 Bill Wyman in '82

12 Gerard Kenny in '78

13 Elvis Costello in '80

14 Hedgehoppers Anonymous in '65

15 Howard Johnson in '82

16 Fantastics in '71

17 Howard Jones in '83

18 Duran Duran in '84

19 Killing Joke in '84

20 Roger Whittaker in '70

There have been many hits that have owed a great deal to television one way or another. This quiz deals with hit singles that have some connection with television.

1　Which TV-AM superstar rapped his way into the charts?

2　Who had a hit with the theme from the TV series *Supergran*?

3　Was it Starsky or Hutch who had two number one hits?

4　Of which show was 'Yellow Pearl' by Philip Lynott the theme?

5　Mike Post and Larry Carlton teamed up for a hit with the theme of which TV cop series?

6　Which TV series brought neil fame?

7　Which other star of that series hit with 'Ullo John, Gotta New Motor'?

8　What was the Firm's hit, inspired by 'Minder'?

9　Clannad have had two TV series theme hits. 'Robin (The Hooded Man)' was one. What was the other?

10　The theme from *Van Der Valk* was a number one hit. What was it called?

11　Which TV-manufactured group hit the top with 'I'm A Believer'?

12　A TV theme stayed at number two for six weeks while John Travolta and Olivia Newton-John held the top spot. What was it?

13　Possibly the most successful TV group of all time were really only one man, yet they certainly cleaned up in 1974. Who were they?

14　Which TV series cast hit with 'Hi-Fidelity' and 'Starmaker'?

15　Corporal Jones from *Dad's Army* hit number one with which song?

16　Which TV megastars (and a frog) took 'Halfway Down The Stairs' more than halfway up the charts?

17　Which TV film included 'I Am The Walrus' by the Beatles

18　What was the theme from *Auf Wiedersehen Pet*?

19　Kenny Everett's TV series caused Sid Snot to make a hit record. What was it?

20　Who hit with the 'Fraggle Rock Theme' early in 1984?

1 Which TV theme did Ken Barrie take into the charts?

2 What Christmas hit did Dennis Waterman and George Cole come up with?

3 Who were the Sergeant Major and Lofty, and what was their number one hit?

4 In which show did Stephanie de Sykes feature 'Born With A Smile On My Face'?

5 What was the biggest hit to emerge from Elvis' TV Special in 1969?

6 Two film themes have reached number one largely as a result of the TV series spin-off. One was 'Fame', but what was the other?

7 Which number one started life as a TV jingle for petrol?

8 Which hit became even more well known as the 'Nimble' bread jingle?

9 Which film theme was used by BBC-TV as their Olympics signature tune in 1984?

10 Which TV cartoon characters hit number one with 'Sugar Sugar'?

11 The theme from the Japanese import series *The Water Margin* was a hit for a Japanese group. Who?

12 What was the theme from Cilla Black's 1968 TV series, written by Paul McCartney?

13 And what was the theme from her series three years later, that climbed to number three?

14 Which number one hit started life as a Coca-Cola TV jingle?

15 Who was the first act to appear 50 times on *Top Of The Pops*?

16 Which TV trio hit with 'Sick Man Blues', 'Wild Thing' and 'Black Pudding Bertha'?

17 Who was the TV reporter whose film from Ethiopia inspired Band Aid?

18 Twelve years after his hit with the theme from *Cade's County*, he came back to the charts with music from *The Thorn Birds*. Who?

19 Which Spanish guitarist took the *Thorn Birds* music into the Top Ten?

20 Which TV family took 'Breaking Up Is Hard To Do' even higher than composer Neil Sedaka did?

1 'Always The Lonely One' was a small hit in 1963 for Alan Drew. In which TV serial did this character appear?

2 Max Harris took the 'Gurney Slade' theme into the charts. Which chart-topper played the title role?

3 Which number one hit took off after being featured in the series *Harpers West One*?

4 Who wrote 'Argentine Melody' by San Jose, the BBC theme for their 1978 World Cup coverage?

5 Roland Rat and Dr Kildare both hit with the same song. What was it?

6 What was the title of the vocal version of the theme from 'Dr Kildare'?

7 Who was the bearded one in Brown Sauce?

8 Perry Como's TV show featured a segment where he sang requests. On one occasion he sang a song sent in by some viewers, and then went on to record the song and take it in to the Top Ten. What was the song?

9 Who recorded 'At The Palace (Parts 1 and 2)'?

10 Which four girls were 'O.K?' in *Rock Follies*?

11 Who hit with 'Theme From Hong Kong Beat'?

12 Which folk singer of the 60s got his first break on *Ready Steady Go*?

13 In which series did Leslie Fyson star, and perform the hit signature tune?

14 Which TV series provided a hit for the Early Music Consort?

15 Of which TV series was 'Whatever Happened To You' the theme?

16 Who plays Mr Humphries and what was his hit single?

17 Who took the 'Maigret Theme' into the Top 20 in 1962?

18 Which orchestra leaders had hits with the *Z Cars* theme?

19 What single by a number one hitmaker – a flop in Britain but a Top 20 hit in the States – spawned a TV mini-series in 1985?

20 A TV theme became the first record to sell a million in Britain without reaching number one. What was it?

<table>
<tr><td>QUIZ 34</td><td>I CALL YOUR NAME</td></tr>
</table>

Twenty years ago, "John, Paul, George and Ringo" was famous long-hand for the Beatles. How many other groups can be identified in the same way? The following lists of names are the line-ups of hitmaking groups at some point of their success. Don't worry about the surnames, just identify the groups.

1 George and Andrew
2 Mick, Keith, Bill, Charlie and Brian
3 Phil and Don
4 Agnetha, Anna-Frid, Bjorn and Benny
5 Eric, Jack and Ginger
6 Richard and Karen
7 George, John, Mikey and Roy
8 Freddie, Brian, John and Roger
9 Paul and Art
10 Eric, Graham, Kevin and Lol
11 Limahl, Nick, Steve, Stuart and Jez
12 Holly, Paul, Mark, Brian and Peter
13 Daryl and John
14 Jimi, Larry and Steve
15 Dave and Annie
16 Chrissie, Pete, Martin and James
17 Tom, Alanna and Joe
18 Diana, Mary and Florence
19 Simon, John, Andy, Roger and Nick
20 Mick, John, Stevie, Lindsey and Christine

1 Tony, Gary, Martin, Steve and John
2 Robert, Jimmy, John and John
3 Buddy, Jerry, Niki and Joe
4 Donald and Walter
5 Phil, Mike and Tony
6 Paul, Mick, Boz and Simon
7 Robbie, Richard, Levon, Garth and Rick
8 Viv, Neil, Roger, Rodney and "Legs" Larry

9   Pete, Roger, John and Keith
10   Brinsley, Nick, Billy, Bob and Ian
11   Patti, Nona and Sarah
12   Davy, Mickey, Mike and Peter
13   Roger, Dave, Nick and Rick
14   Mary, Paul and Peter
15   Ruth, Anita and June
16   John, Michelle, Cass and Denny
17   John, Zal, Steve and Joe
18   David, Eddie, Paul, Otis and Melvin
19   Alan and Georgie
20   Keith, Greg and Carl

1   Alan, Hamish, Onnie, Robbie, Roger and Malcolm
2   John, Tom, Doug and Stu
3   David, Stephen, Graham and Neil
4   Ronald, Rudolph and Kelly
5   Ace, Paul, Gene and Pete
6   Lowell, Bill, Richard, Paul, Sam and Kenny
7   Tim, Janis, Alan and Laurel
8   Geoff and Trevor
9   Dan, Manny, Pete and Darryl
10   Felix, Eddie, Dino and Gene
11   Kazuhiko, Rei, Yukihiro, Mika, Masayoshi and Hiroshi
12   Jim and Dash
13   Maybelle, June, Helen and Anita
14   Les, Dave, Rob and Roy
15   Bob, Dave and Nick
16   Billy, Dusty and Frank
17   Roebuck, Cleotha, Mavis and Yvonne
18   Ron, Florence, Billy, Lamonte and Marilyn
19   Lester and Earl
20   Maxene, Patti and LaVerne

ALL THOSE YEARS AGO

Listed below are song titles from the 70s. One word has been omitted from each title, all you have to do is find that one word.

1 '. . . . . . Water' – Four Tops
2 '. . . . . . Chile' – Jimi Hendrix
3 'Kung Fu . . . . . .' – Carl Douglas
4 'Swing Your . . . . . .' – Jim Gilstrap
5 '. . . . . . Better Change' – Stranglers
6 '. . . . . . On' – Floaters
7 'Ma . . . . . .' – Boney M
8 'Shooting . . . . . .' – Dollar
9 'A Walkin' . . . . . .' – Limmie and the Family Cookin'
10 'All The Young . . . . . .' – Mott The Hoople

1 '. . . . . . Song' – Alan Price
2 '. . . . . . Baby' – Helen Reddy
3 '. . . . . . So Good' – Susan Cadogan
4 '. . . . . . Lightnin'' – John Travolta
5 'I Love . . . . . .' – Patrick Juvet
6 'Germ-Free . . . . . .' – X-Ray Spex
7 'Sound Of The . . . . . .' – Members
8 '. . . . . . Party' – Paul Nicholas
9 'Pepper . . . . . .' – Peppers
10 'I . . . . . . Love You' – Olivia Newton-John

1 'Vaya Con . . . . . .' – Millican and Nesbit
2 '. . . . . . Day' – Father Abraham and the Smurfs
3 '. . . . . . Girl' – Smokie
4 'Take On The . . . . . .' – Judas Priest
5 '. . . . . . Rider' – War
6 '. . . . . . Tune' – Andy Fairweather-Low
7 '. . . . . . Overture' – Electric Light Orchestra
8 'Sister . . . . . .' – New World
9 'Monkey . . . . . .' – Dave and Ansil Collins
10 'Don't You . . . . . .' – Butterscotch

JACK AND DIANE

This quiz is in the form of a coded conversation between Jack and Diane. Listed below are a number of clues, each one leading to the title of a hit single. When all the titles are put together in the order given, they turn into a complete, if rather short, story. Award yourself two points for each clue successfully deciphered.

That is not all. The initial letters of the first word of the answers to the clues marked with an asterisk (*) form an anagram. When correctly arranged this will give you the name of the recording act that hit with the answer to the clue marked #. This is worth three more points. You may find that the use of *British Hit Singles, 5th edition* is essential to find out all the answers, so go out and buy one first.

(ABBA's follow-up to 'Waterloo')

Bachelors' only chart-topper: Lionel Richie's solo number one

Ultravox's fourth Top 20 hit: Easybeats' follow-up to 'Friday On My Mind'. Manfred Mann's hit about the Greta Garbo Home for Wayward Boys and Girls*. Fleetwood Mac's early 1983 Top Ten disc/Stevie's Oscar-winning Wonder-hit.

163rd British number one: Bruce Channel's Mercury hit/a hit for both Marvin Gaye and Junior Walker/Nina Simone's Bee Gees hit*/Brook Benton's biggest*/Shirley Bassey's 50s chart-topper.

The man in the sand in the Isle of Man: Herman's only solo hit! Top Ten hit three times, for Dusty, Elvis and Guys and Dolls. Perry Como hit, but Barbara George missed with this title/Adam Faith's 18th hit.

Con, Dec and John's only number one:	First British hit for a Cher duettist#/Boney M's first hit to miss the Top 50. Barry White's third Top Ten hit/Philip Bailey's group's first hit in the UK
The Who's last Reaction hit:	Flip side of 'Day Tripper'/Flip side of 'Bachelor Boy'/Felice Taylor's only hit. Bellamy Brothers' 1979 top three hits/Hot Chocolate hit kept from the top by 'Bohemian Rhapsody'.
Bachelors' second Top Ten hit:	Commodores' 13th hit*/Carly Simon hit helped by Mick Jagger. Tami Lynn's two-time hit/Johnnie Ray's fifth hit/James and Bobby Purify's classic, and biggest, hit. Sex Pistols cover of a Monkees US hit. Film theme and Four Aces biggest UK hit*. Vertigo QUO 3/Gaye and Terrell's second chart entry*/Alternate title for 'Alternate Title'.
Rolling Stones' seventh number one:	Ray Charles classic hit for Jerry Lee Lewis/both Lennon and McCartney wrote separate hits with this title. Frankie Lymon's second hit. Spencer Davis Group's last and Chicago's first Top Ten hit/Perry Como's Don McLean-written hit*. Shirelles hit reworked by Melanie.
Bachelors' only US Top Ten hit:	Mike Sarne hit with Billie Davis
Scott Walker's first solo hit:	Glitter and Big Ben Banjo Bands both hit with this title/Atomic Rooster's first hit. Nancy Sinatra's follow-up to 'Boots'.

First Irish number one since 'Softly Softly':

Shaky's favourite of his hits but not a number one! Cyndi Lauper's chart debut/Genesis Christmas '83 chart entry. Phil Collins number one/Jimmy Soul's American number one. A hit for both Shirley Bassey and Connie Francis/Nilsson's number one.

Number one from 19 June 1968:

Sonny and Cher's second Atlantic hit......

Last Irish chart-topper before 'Rat Trap':

Singalongamax's last Top Ten hit*. Ray Charles' first UK Top Tenner. Peter Cook and Dudley Moore's only hit.

"Gordon is a Moron":

The Orlons' only UK hit. Them's first hit. The other side of Elvis Presley's 'I Beg Of You'

(Simon and Garfunkel's first US hit – which flopped in Britain)

Sade's third hit: Hall and Oates' first hit.

| THREE STARS

This is a quiz about threesomes – questions about trios or about songs that are about trios or about records that have some tenuous connection with the number three.

Complete the following trios:

1 Peter, Paul and –
2 'Shake, Rattle and –'
3 'Me and You and a Dog named –'
4 Emerson, Lake and –
5 Earth, Wind and –

Identify these:

6 Three Americans, not real brothers, who based themselves in the UK, scoring number ones here in 1965 and 1966
7 A trio (one Brit, two Yanks) who added a Canadian for a time – surprisingly, their only two US Top Ten hits occurred in 1977 and 1982 when they were back to a trio again
8 The first to be called a super-group; two out of the three became half of Blind Faith
9 Siobhan, Sarah and Karen
10 'New York Mining Disaster 1941' was a hit for them when they were a fivesome
11 Style Council forerunners
12 Invisible Sunbathers
13 The man who warbled '1–2–3' back in '65
14 A German three-man group with remarkably unimaginative name
15 A hit of the above German group which consisted of one word (or at least a kind of word) thrice
16 A group who equalled a 21-year-old record set by Gerry and The Pacemakers when their third single became their third number one
17 A group whose *amour* was a lady three times over
18 A trio of Twins
19 Now down to three, these black sisters got so excited in 1984
20 Diana, Florence and Mary

Complete the following threesomes:

1 'Veni, Vidi, –'
2 Dino, Desi and –
3 Hamilton, Joe Frank and –
4 Kenny Rogers, Kim Carnes and –
5 Diana Ross and The Supremes and –

Who sang:

6 'Go, Go, Go'
7 'Fun, Fun, Fun'
8 'Money, Money, Money'
9 'Gimme, Gimme, Gimme (A Man After Midnight)'
10 'Hi Hi Hi'

Identify these:

11 The first to sing 'Be My Baby'
12 Ronnie, Nedra and Estelle
13 This group had one of the masters of popular music. Usually a fivesome but recorded their most successful album as a trio in Nigeria
14 Had a double-sided hit in 1975 with 'Nappy Love' and a revival of a Troggs smash
15 Britain's most popular sisters in the fifties
16 Harmony songwriting/singing group who hit with 'Funny How Love Can Be' in 1965
17 Ashley, Leee and Errol
18 US group, based in the UK, who hit first with 'Runaway Boys' in 1980
19 The only number one for Eddie Cochran
20 The writers of 'I Know Him So Well'

1 Which girl trio had their only Top Ten UK hit in 1958 with a song that regretted a birthday?
2 Which trio were the second Irish act to top the UK charts, a decade after Ruby Murray, the first?
3 Which duo gave Johnny Cash support on several of his recordings thus making the billed artistes on the label a trio?

4   Who did not chart in the UK with Motown classics 'Needle In A Haystack' and 'He Was Really Saying Something' but did with the less well-remembered 'These Things Will Keep Me Loving You'?

5   Which trio had one American hit entitled 'Yogi' and a name similar to the answer to B 16 above?

6   Who were Bob Shane, Nick Reynolds and Dave Guard?

7   Who covered Leo Sayer's first British success and had a number four hit in the US with it?

8   Who released an album in 1984 entitled 'Grace Under Pressure'?

9   Who wrote 'I Feel Love' with Pete Bellotte and Donna Summer?

10 Who had a minor 1984 hit with a revival of Buddy Knox's 'Party Doll'?

11 Which femme has had three UK number ones in conjunction with other acts (two with one, one with the other), yet none as a solo performer?

12 Who was the first UK act to have three number one hits with consecutive releases?

13 Who were featured on TSOP with MFSB?

14 Which major chart act of 1984 first hit in their home country (America) with 'Francene' back in 1972?

15 Who helped out the Cornelius Brothers?

16 Which Liverpudlian trio, rated by many as one of the best groups to emerge during the Merseybeat boom, only made number 22 with their biggest hit entitled 'By The Way'?

17 Who became a trio when John's brother Tom left?

18 Who stole much of the thunder from Les Compagnons De La Chanson in 1959?

19 Who was grateful for the Aintree Iron?

20 Which three Stewarts have had Top Ten UK hits as Stewarts? (i.e. Dave Stewart of the Eurythmics does not count)

<table>
<tr><td>QUIZ 38</td><td>(CALL ME) NUMBER ONE</td></tr>
</table>

This quiz is about artists and records that have topped the various American charts in *Billboard* **during 1984–5.**

1 What was Van Halen's first number one single?
2 What single was helped to number one by a video featuring a blind girl?
3 What was Kenny Loggins' chart-topping film theme?
4 On what number one album did The Revolution first perform?
5 Who leads the group The News?
6 What was Culture Club's first American number one?
7 Who was the writer and producer of Ray Parker Jr.'s 'Ghostbusters'?
8 What number one album spawned seven Top Ten singles between 1982 and 1984?
9 What was Wham's first American number one?
10 What number one appeared in the film *The Woman in Red*?
11 Who wrote USA For Africa's 'We Are The World'?
12 Whose face was shown on the front cover of Phil Collins' *No Jacket Required*?
13 Who duetted with Willie Nelson on the country number one 'To All The Girls I've Loved Before'?
14 What was Madonna's first number one?
15 What two men made the number one album *Make It Big*?
16 What was the biggest hit single from Bruce Springsteen's *Born in the USA*?

1 Ashford and Simpson had a number one black music hit with 'Solid'. What are their first names?
2 What was Bronski Beat's number one dance hit?
3 What was Foreigner's biggest hit before their number one 'I Want To Know What Love Is'?
4 Who wrote Diana Ross' black music list leader 'Missing You'?
5 While 'Pipes Of Peace' was number one in Britain Paul McCartney also had number one in America. With what song?

6   What was Cyndi Lauper's number one from *She's So Unusual*?

7   Who was the first British black to reach number one on the Hot 100?

8   'Can't Fight This Feeling' was REO Speedwagon's comeback hit. What was their first number one?

9   Maze reached the top of the black music chart with 'Back In Stride'. Who is their front man?

10 Who wrote and produced the Mary Jane Girls' dance number one 'In My House'?

11 What was the first single release from *Purple Rain*?

12 On what US label did Duran Duran's 'The Reflex' appear?

13 John Waite of 'Missing You' fame had previously reached the top twenty with what group?

14 To what two artists did the Commodores' black music number one 'Nightshift' pay tribute?

15 What was Andrew Lloyd Webber's number one classical album?

16 What number one album featured the track 'The Heart Of Rock And Roll'?

1   What was the artist billing on American copies of 'Careless Whisper'?

2   A single produced by Trevor Horn reached number one in America during 1984. What was it?

3   'What's Love Got To Do With It' was Tina Turner's first number one. In what year had she first charted with husband Ike?

4   In what number one did the artist sing about visiting a psychoanalyst in California?

5   Who played the sax solo on Phil Collins' 'One More Night'?

6   Deniece Williams scaled the summit with 'Let's Hear It For The Boy'. With what song had she been there previously?

7   What was Daryl Hall and John Oates' number one from *Big Bam Boom*?

8   Who performed the number one dance hit 'Bad Habits'?

9   With whom did Ray Charles have a number one country duet?

10 What historic feat did Patti Labelle and Harold Faltermeyer perform together?

11 Sheila E. had a number one dance hit with 'The Glamorous Life'. What does the "E" stand for?

12 Who sang lead on 'Can't Fight This Feeling'?

13 What single by Chaka Khan that did not become a big pop hit did go to number one on the dance chart?

14 Willie Nelson's 'The City Of New Orleans' was a posthumous country number one for what songwriter?

15 What number one album featured the track 'Inside Out'?

16 In what chart group did Sheila E.'s father perform?

QUIZ 39	STAR ON A TV SHOW

All these questions refer to TV Music Programmes

1 Which pop TV programme began life in January 1964?

2 Which pop TV programme did Generation X sing about?

3 On which show did teenage record critic Janice Nichols rise to stardom with her now classic phrase "Oi'll give it foive"?

4 Which programme was co-presented for a while by actress Lesley Ash?

5 Which punk orientated pop show featured satirist Peter Cook?

6 On which pop TV programme did Duran Duran and Spandau Ballet play against each other?

7 For which programme was 'Stone Fox Chase' the theme?

8 Marty Wilde was the resident star of this Jack Good-produced pop show

9 Which TV show was co-hosted by Pete Murray and Jo Douglas and boxer Freddie Mills?

10 What is the O.R.S.?

1 Which TV pop show competition was won by the Bo Street Runners?

2 Which ITV pop series ran for 3 years and featured Stevi Merike, Kid Jensen and Mike Read as respective hosts?

3 What is the link between John Barry and David Jacobs?

4 Which cartoonist/saxophonist hosted BBC 1's *Whole Scene Going*?

5 What is the link between Alistair Pirie and Quincy Jones?

6 Alan Freeman was the regular host of which late 60s BBC 1 pop show?

7   Which lady presenter hosted *Saturday Scene*?

8   In June 1964 Southern TV screened the first ever TV Pop Quiz: what was it called?

9   Which DJ hosted BBC 1's 75 minute look back over the previous decade on New Year's Eve 1969?

10 Who conceived the legendary pop documentary 'All My Loving'?

1   Who hosted Southern TV's *New Release* show screened in most areas in the late 60s?

2   In July 1969 LWT shot a pilot for what was intended to be TV's first pop underground series. It was the brainchild of a member of which chart-topping group?

3   To coincide with the landing of the Apollo II spacecraft on the moon, an ITV marathon, compered by David Frost and starring artists such as Cliff Richard, Lulu, Cilla Black and Engelbert Humperdink, was screened on Sunday, 20 July 1969. What was the show called?

4   From which country did the pop series *Stramash* originate?

5   Before 'Hit and Miss', what was the original theme to BBC 1's *Juke Box Jury*?

6   Pop singer, Ian Whitcomb, who became a star in America in the mid-60s with his hit record 'You Turn Me On', was one of the original presenters on which British TV show?

7   In August 1959 which pop series that included The Raindrops and Bob Miller's Millermen amongst its resident artists came to the end of its run?

8   In which pop programme did Spike Milligan perform sketches?

9   When one early pop programme released an album from the show, Cliff Richard couldn't make the photo call for the LP cover and was replaced by Duffy Power. What was the show?

10 Which successful pop show came off the screen in June 1966?

STRANGE BREW

In each group of names listed in this quiz, there is one odd man out. For example, in the first group of Roland Orzabal, Boy George and Jon Moss, the odd one out is Roland Orzabal, who is not part of Culture Club. Choosing Boy George as the only one who does not use his surname, or as the only one on show in Madame Tussauds would be wrong. We are not trying to be too clever by half, at least not in sections A and B.

1   Roland Orzabal, Boy George, Jon Moss
2   George Michael, David Ball, Andrew Ridgeley
3   Elton John, Howard Jones, Paul Young
4   'She Loves You', 'Let It Be', 'Penny Lane'
5   'Union Of The Snake', 'Rio', 'The Reflex'
6   Alison Moyet, Cyndi Lauper, Tina Turner
7   Ringo Starr, Stewart Copeland, Brian May
8   *No Jacket Required, No Parlez, The Secret Of Association*
9   'One Night In Bangkok', 'Queen For Tonight', 'I Know Him So Well'
10   Big Bopper, Big Dee Irwin, Little Richard
11   Michael Jackson, Stevie Wonder, Lionel Richie
12   Eurythmics, Frankie Goes To Hollywood, ABC, Art Of Noise
13   Marc and the Mambas, Python Lee Jackson, Yellow Dog
14   'Penny Lane', 'Please Please Me', 'Let It Be'
15   'Hungry Like The Wolf', 'Save A Prayer', 'Rio', 'Girls On Film'
16   Thelma Houston, Mary Wells, Kim Weston, Tammi Terrell
17   'How Do You Do It', 'I Like It', 'You'll Never Walk Alone', 'I'm The One'
18   Randy, Wanda, Marlon, LaToya, Tito
19   'School's Out'/'Relax!', 'Je T'Aime . . . Moi Non Plus', 'Tell Laura I Love Her'
20   'Ashes To Ashes', 'Space Oddity', 'The Jean Genie', 'Let's Dance'

1. 'Little Red Rooster', 'Satisfaction', 'It's All Over Now'
2. Jona Lewie, Jonathan King, Terry Dactyl
3. RCA, Columbia, Parlophone
4. 'Love Me Do', 'All My Loving', 'Do You Want To Know A Secret'
5. Pete Best, Jimmy Nicol, Billy Preston, Ringo Starr
6. Fox, Yazoo, Platters
7. Yardbirds, Spencer Davis Group, Cream
8. Barry Gibb, Maurice Gibb, Robin Gibb
9. 'Back Home', 'Blue Is The Colour', 'Nice One Cyril'
10. Stevie Wonder, Cliff Richard, Elton John, Elvis Presley, Billy Fury, George Michael
11. Temperance Seven, Peter Sellers, America, Beatles, Searchers
12. 'We Are The World', 'Welcome To The Pleasuredome', 'Pie Jesu'
13. Sakkarin, 53rd and 3rd, Piglets
14. 'Answer Me', 'I See The Moon', 'This Ole House'
15. Sonny and Cher, Ike and Tina Turner, Nino Tempo and April Stevens
16. Go West, Go-Gos, Duran Duran, Talk Talk
17. Barry Gibb, Ray Davies, Peter Sarstedt, Billy Fury
18. Floaters, Elaine Paige and Barbara Dickson, Nicole, Jerry Keller
19. Bill Wyman, Jack Bruce, Les Chadwick, John McNally
20. 'Day Tripper', 'Hello Goodbye', 'Eleanor Rigby'

1. Bob Dylan, David Bowie, Boomtown Rats, Kool and the Gang
2. Big Dee Irwin, Steve Miller, Meat Loaf
3. Elvis Presley, Cliff Richard, Gene Pitney, Marianne Faithfull, Devo
4. 'Proud Mary', 'City Of New Orleans', 'Wreck Of The Edmund Fitzgerald'
5. Freddie Garrity, Freddie Marsden, Freddie Mercury
6. Byrds, Monkees, Manfred Mann, Rolling Stones
7. Cliff Richard, Elvis Presley, Andy Williams, Lonnie Donegan
8. Marty Wilde, Dodie Stevens, Tommy Edwards
9. Helmut Zacharias, Tommy Zang, Georghe Zamfir
10. Michael Jackson, Dinah Washington, Ryan Paris, Julie London

11   Norway, Sweden, Finland, Denmark
12   New York Dolls, Detroit Wheels, Buffalo Springfield
13   Manfred Mann, John McVie, Eric Clapton, Peter Green, Aynsley Dunbar
14   Cheynes, Downliners Sect, Fleetwood Mac
15   Johnny Preston, Marvin Rainwater, Kay Starr, Cher
16   Rah Band, Real Thing, Olivia Newton-John, Damned, Lulu
17   *Duke, Abacab, A Trick Of The Tail*
18   'Rock On', 'Goodbye', 'Hot Love', 'America'
19   Rolling Stones, Hollies, Ray Charles, Earth Wind and Fire
20   Dee Dee Sharp, Archie Bell, O'Jays, Billy Paul, Three Degrees, Lou Rawls

| QUIZ 41 | PRIZE OF GOLD |

These questions are all about Grammy Award winners. Remember that an artist's award is for the previous year's achievement, since ceremonies are held the year after the records have been released.

1   Debby Boone won Best New Artist of 1977. It turned out she had already had her biggest hit. What was it?
2   What Record of the Year by Bobby Darin had previously been a US and UK hit for Louis Armstrong?
3   Christopher Cross won the most statuettes at the 1981 ceremonies. What was his Record of the Year?
4   Who won Best New Artist in 1985?
5   Who won a Best Female Country Performance award for 'Stand By Your Man'?
6   1976 New Artist of the Year Starland Vocal Band had only one major hit. What was it?
7   Who wrote the 1971 Song of the Year, 'You've Got A Friend'?
8   The Best Jazz Performance of 1965, 'The "In" Crowd' by the Ramsey Lewis Trio, became the signature tune of what BBC Radio 1 DJ?
9   Tina Turner won Grammy Awards in 1985 for 'What's Love Got To Do With It' and what rock record?
10   The Beatles won a Best Soundtrack Grammy for what 1970 film?
11   Where did Tony Bennett leave his heart, according to the 1962 Record of the Year?

12 Aretha Franklin won the Best Female R&B Vocal Performance for eight consecutive years until Natalie Cole broke her streak with what hit?

13 The first rock record to win Album of the Year was *Sgt. Pepper's Lonely Hearts Club Band*. In what year was it released?

14 What British group won Best New Artist at the 1984 ceremonies?

15 Who performed the 1976 Record of the Year, 'This Masquerade'?

16 Norman Whitfield won a Best Soundtrack Grammy for what film score featuring performances by Rose Royce?

17 Who has won more Grammy awards than any other artist?

18 Roberta Flack won Record of the Year for both 1972 and 1973. Her first winner was 'The First Time Ever I Saw Your Face'. What was the second?

19 What film gave Percy Faith a Grammy-winning film theme?

20 What vocalist won a Grammy with the Lieber-Stoller song 'Is That All There Is'?

1 Who wrote the 1984 Song of the Year 'What's Love Got To Do With It'?

2 Domenico Modugno won Record of the Year at the first Grammy Awards with 'Nel Blu Dipinto Di Blu'. By what subtitle is this song better known?

3 The first Album of the Year was *Music From Peter Gunn*. Who was the artist?

4 Judy Garland won Album of the Year in 1961 with a live recording. What was the famous venue?

5 *The Concert for Bangla Desh* won 1972 Album of the Year. Name at least five artists on the record.

6 In 1976 Paul Simon accepted his Album of the Year award by thanking Stevie Wonder, winner the previous two years, for not releasing an LP that year. Stevie won again the year after with what long player?

7 For what single did Sam and Dave win their only Grammy?

8 Soeur Sourire won the 1963 Best Gospel or Other Religious Recording trophy for what hit?

9 'It's Too Late' by Carole King was the 1971 Record of the Year. What record executive produced it?

10 Bruce Johnston penned the 1976 Song of the Year 'I Write The Songs'. Who had the UK hit version?

11 George Martin won an Arrangement Grammy for what 1973 Wings hit?

12 What two men who have charted as solo artists co-wrote the Doobie Brothers' 1979 Record of the Year 'What A Fool Believes'?

13 Harry Nilsson has won two Best Male Vocal Performance awards, one for 'Everybody's Talkin''. For what single did he win the other?

14 Who won the 1974 Producer of the Year designation for work that included hits by the Spinners and Stylistics?

15 The 1964 Record of the Year was 'The Girl From Ipanema'. Who played tenor sax?

16 Whose version of 'Up Up And Away' was named 1967 Record of the Year?

17 The Beatles were Best New Artist of 1964. What was their first US chart entry?

18 'Send In The Clowns' won the 1975 Song of the Year. Who wrote it?

19 What multiple Grammy winner was credited with a *Button Down Mind*?

20 Barbra Streisand won Best Female Vocal Performance three years running, twice for LPs and once for her first US Top Ten single. What was the 45?

1 Michael Jackson's Grammy sweep in 1984 included one category that had nothing to do with *Thriller*. What was it?

2 'The Battle Of New Orleans' was 1959s Song of the Year. Who wrote it?

3 'Strangers In The Night' by Frank Sinatra was the 1966 Record of the Year. What former artist produced the disc?

4 In an infamous Best New Artist poll Elvis Costello and the Cars were both beaten by what act?

5 Ernest Gold won the 1960 Song of the Year award with 'Theme From *Exodus*'. Who had the hit version?

6 Who was Ernest Gold's hit-making son?

7 The Best Rock and Roll Recording category only survived four years. Most of the winners could not be remotely considered rock and roll. For example, Bent Fabric won for a 1962 instrumental. What was it?

8 Marvin Hamlisch won a bizarre triple for 1974, taking home trophies for Best New Artist, Song of the Year and Best Instrumental Performance. What was his piano hit?

9 What was the Song of the Year Hamlisch co-wrote with Marilyn and Alan Bergman?

10 Who showed their versatility by winning a 1974 Country Grammy for 'Fairytale'?

11 Who won the 1974 Best Engineered Record trophy for *Band on the Run*?

12 The annotator of Bob Dylan's *Blood on the Tracks* won a 1975 Best Album Notes Grammy but had his work deleted from later printings of the LP sleeve. Who was the hapless hero?

13 Peter Nero was named 1961's Best New Artist. What instrument did he play?

14 'Color Him Father' won the 1969 Best R&B Song award for writer Richard Spencer. Who took the song to the US Top Ten?

15 The follow-up to 'Color Him Father' was a hit single for Paul Young years later. Name it.

16 What was the Kendalls' 1977 Grammy-winning country hit?

17 What Album of the Year was produced by Richard Pashut and Ken Caillat?

18 Quincy Jones won his first Grammy for arranging what Ray Charles classic?

19 What is the first name of the Grammy-winning instrumentalist Deodato?

20 Who won the first Best Performance by an Orchestra award with *Billy May's Big Fat Brass*?

Here are three lists of 31 names or words that are extremely familiar to all students of popular music. These 31 are in fact 15 pairs of names or words plus one outsider. Your job is to identify the outsider by pairing off the other 30. Pairs could be "Elvis" and "Presley" or "Simon" and "Garfunkel" or even "Heart" and "Soul" – you'll soon catch on.

A	B	C
Elvis	Johnny	Years After
Lulu	Sid	Love
Lewis	Duran	Benny
McCartney	Bobby McGee	Ace
Gordon	Boy	Elaine
Gambaccini	Wood	Paul
Dee	Wood	Jacks
Dave	Sid	Barbra
Scritti	Renee	Jonathan
Pete	Paul	Randy
Benny	Me	Bohemian
Luvvers	Le Bon	Ten
Linda	Williams	Pride
Paul	Duran	Tudor
Presley	Ron	Rhapsody
Peter	Jeremy	Barbra
Paul	George	Five
Politti	George	King
Julian	Simon	Jackson
Roll	Roy	King
Julian	Rotten	Neil
Paul	Terry	Terry
Dave	Renato	Barbara
Hank	Andy	Ten Pole
Björn	Simon	C.C.
Clark	Vicious	Kefford
Lloyd Webber	Hissing	Jets
Bruce	Michael	Queen
Rock	Jackson	Ten
Lennon	Chad	Donna
Hardcastle	Joe	Jackson

CALLING YOUR NAME

The answers to all these questions are names.

1 Paul Anka's number one lady
2 Michael Jackson's 'Thriller' girl
3 Rod Stewart's number one lady
4 ABBA could hear his drums
5 The Four Pennies were her Romeos
6 Scaffold's Pink Lady
7 Kenny Rogers' number one woman
8 Little Richard and the Everly Brothers all escorted her into the Top Ten
9 "Hello", said Louis Armstrong, Kenny Ball, Frank Sinatra and Frankie Vaughan
10 Ken Barrie's Postman
11 The other side of Jam's 'A-Bomb in Wardour Street'
12 Brotherhood Of Man's first number one man
13 Brotherhood Of Man's second number one man
14 "Come on", said Dexy
15 Paper Lace told him not to be a hero
16 Derek and the Dominoes' girl
17 Siouxsie's dear girl
18 Who Greg Lake believes in
19 David Bowie and Peter Schilling both sang about this major
20 He can play a guitar like ringing a bell

1 Toto's Top 20 girl
2 Clannad's hooded man
3 Human League saw her at the bus stop
4 Kool and the Gang's 14th hit was their biggest to date
5 Steely Dan and Tom Robinson told him not to lose that number
6 Alexei Sayle asked if he'd purchased a new vehicle recently
7 The Smiths told him it was really nothing
8 Cilla Black asked him what's it all about
9 The leader of Elton John's Jets
10 Dawn's first girl

11 Creedence's proud one
12 Elton John's older brother, leaving tonight on a plane
13 Blondie sang about him in English and French
14 Hot Chocolate tried to make her a star of the silver screen
15 David Bowie told him he was only dancing (again) (in 1972 and 1975)
16 Ray Davies said he was a man, and so was she
17 The Overlanders' French Beatle girl
18 Toni Basil thinks he's so fine
19 "Oh", sang Neil Sedaka
20 "Oh", sang Fleetwood Mac

1 Rick Springfield loved his girl
2 Peter Cook sang his ballad
3 Marianne Faithfull sang her ballad
4 Duane Eddy twanged his ballad
5 The Goodies' Black Pudding lady
6 Shane Fenton said that today was her birthday
7 Orchestral Manoeuvres in the Dark's atomic bomber
8 Jim Dale wrote it and the Seekers sang the theme from a Lynn Redgrave film
9 Ruby Murray sang "goodbye" to him, "goodbye"
10 Bob Wallis told her he was shy
11 Department S asked if he was there in 1981
12 Dolly Parton begged her, "please don't take my man"
13 Roy Orbison spent nine weeks with her on the UK singles chart in 1966
14 Sue Thompson asked him to hold the ladder steady
15 Perez Prado took her to number eight in '58 (and to number one in the States)
16 Chipmunks' ragtime cowboy
17 Peter E. Bennett had a seagull
18 The man with the amazing dancing bear
19 The guitarist in the Sultans Of Swing who knows all the chords
20 For whom the Three Bells tolled

A LITTLE BIT MORE

This entertaining little batch of teasers is the reverse of the witty quiz number 19. Instead of one letter being deleted from each star's name to create a whole new meaning, one has been added. Example: "Atmosphere singer needs support" would be "Truss Abbott".

(these are all acts who charted in 1984):

1 Dominating lady insect
2 Soft Celler on the parade ground
3 The group have all received their money
4 Old sea-dog in San Damiano
5 Smooth operator keeping out of the sun
6 60s come-back girl keeps her head covered
7 Conversation between plants
8 Jab Baby Jane's creator
9 Canadian heavy-metal broom
10 Berry Gordy's son looks good in a dress
11 Definitely Chris
12 Reg Dwight taking wise precautions when he drives
13 Geldof and Co won't stop talking
14 A fresh edge for 'Blue Monday' boys
15 Ghostbusting donkey
16 Departing from Susanna
17 Car wash experts never use rhyme
18 Former lead Supreme annoyed
19 'I Feel Love' superstar living in squalor
20 Breakaway restaurant car

(all acts from the 70s charts)

1 Elton John's number one colleague becomes a serious thinker
2 Wrecked Mars Bar for Errol's group
3 Insatiable wild side walker
4 'When I Need You' singer teams up with Mark Anthony's love
5 McCartney's playground group
6 Bent version of Eric Burdon's former partners

7   He ain't gonna bump with a big fat woman but may with cooking fat
8   'Hey Girl Don't Bother Me' crew on new lines
9   Insufferably proud about 'I Can Help'
10 Every bit of the 'Year Of The Cat' man
11 Metal act from Copenhagen
12 Arrogant 'Brown-Eyed Girl' singer
13 Steinman protege intended to be in the bread
14 Northern Sri Lankan running away from you
15 He believes in Father Christmas but he's tired
16 Friend who is tired of being alone
17 Sex-mad Bee Gee brother
18 Not quite all of 'Bright Eyes' chanter
19 'Satisfaction' revivers go all county
20 Knobbly mother Baker

(all acts from the 60s charts)

1   South Kensington, Gloucester Road, Hammersmith Broadway, Tottenham Court Road
2   Neck problems for 'Hello Mary Lou' man
3   Mr Bono and applause
4   Strange conductor who hit with 'Caribbean Honeymoon'
5   'My Guy' girl getting larger
6   Aladdin sidekick big in Tulsa
7   Stabbed at her own party
8   'Speedy Gonzales' and foie gras
9   'Dizzy' and highly-strung
10 Soul duo with little to distinguish them from each other
11 Mountaineering warbler of minor chart hits 'You're The Top Cha' and 'Blue-Eyed Boy'
12 TV show for under-fives featuring 'Tip-Toe Through The Tulips'
13 Van Morrison's team go well with Cliff's 1961 Dream
14 Bragging about bell-bottom trousers early in the morning
15 'Rubber Ball' man tends to go off in strange directions
16 Group from 2525 with penchant for French mineral water
17 '1–2–3' gent has been borrowed
18 Whiter than white surfing kings
19 Outbreak of honey-making ganders in Massachusetts
20 Left his heart and money in San Francisco

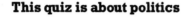

QUIZ 45	PARTY PARTY

This quiz is about politics

1 What was the Beat's advice to Mrs Thatcher?

2 What American President was mentioned in 'Life In A Northern Town'?

3 Neil Kinnock appeared in the video of what song?

4 What Prime Minister was named in a Cream album title?

5 What political system did the Sex Pistols recommend for Britain?

6 What defence minister did the Highwaymen advise to row the boat ashore?

7 They came to take what chart emperor away?

8 According to the Associates, the Tories were afraid of both Labour and the Alliance

9 How did Alice Cooper want to take power?

10 In what Beatles song did John Lennon speculate as to whether a member of the House of Lords had died?

11 What Marvin Gaye hit honoured Presidents Lincoln and Kennedy?

12 Bob Dylan went to Mrs Thatcher's country place

13 Rosemary Clooney marvelled at the age of the Commons

14 Of what group was Janis Joplin lead singer?

15 What political organization did Elvis Presley celebrate in a 1957 hit?

16 These politicians represented the sound of the suburbs

17 What grant of political authority did John Lennon recommend?

18 In what song did the Temptations promise "Vote for me and I'll set you free"?

19 Billy Bragg pledged to support any government that gave a man a living wage in what hit?

20 Madness thought broadcasts from the Commons were quite amusing

1   Frankie Vaughan loved his Prime Minister's flowers
2   What 1984 American Presidential candidate did Melle Mel support?
3   What group advised dissidents to 'Tear The Roof Off The Sucker (Give Up The Funk)'?
4   The Animals envisioned a parliament with Japanese members
5   The Cockerel Chorus admired a Liberal MP
6   What Peter, Paul and Mary hit was the favourite song of Harold Wilson's wife Mary?
7   Rod Stewart claimed that even the President has to have some excitement in what 1980 single?
8   The Four Seasons chirped to Reagan
9   Chicago paid tribute to which American President?
10 Who would the founders of the SDP's favourite group probably be?
11 In what song did Bob Dylan urge senators and congressmen to heed the call?
12 With her name, Mrs Wilson could have been a member of this group
13 It would be a shame, shame, shame if Mrs Williams and the SDP didn't like this act.
14 Harry Secombe wanted global power
15 Stevie Wonder sang about 'Big Brother' on what album?
16 Did Billy Joel dedicate this song to Prime Minister Eden?
17 What group had an American Top 20 hit with 'Farmer John'?
18 Lonnie Donegan took us inside the White House with what hit?
19 The Boomtown Rats saw the Lords in flames
20 Frank Sinatra recalled Prime Minister Ramsay

1 When asked if he thought Margaret Thatcher should appear in a video, Neil Kinnock suggested which song?

2 General Andrew "Old Hickory" Jackson, later President of the United States, was featured in what 1959 smash?

3 What was the name of Vaughn Meader's million-selling Kennedy parody?

4 What 1962 Jimmy Dean single could describe supporters of the Liberal leader?

5 Commander Cody and His Lost Planet Airmen took a ride in what auto named after a US President?

6 Was this 1968 Los Pop Tops release a plea to the upper chamber?

7 Could Count Basie's only US number one have been advice to Nixon?

8 What Cabinet position did James Brown create for himself?

9 What Kingston Trio single endorsed a candidate in a Boston, Massachusetts election?

10 What Stiff album contained two sides of nothing?

11 What executives recorded the 1970 soul smash '5–10–15–20 (25–30 Years Of Love)'?

12 Was Lonnie Donegan's last Top Tenner also a requiem for the Whigs?

13 What 1960 US Top Thirty dance hit honoured the fourth American President?

14 What solon scored with a parody of the Troggs' 'Wild Thing'?

15 What Russ Conway hit paid tribute to senior party members?

16 Millie thought President Taft got fat from eating candy

17 Lita Roza knew back in 1956 what life would be like for Carter once he left office

18 The Village Stompers thought America's first President unhip

19 John Stewart paid tribute to what American politician on his album *California Bloodlines*?

20 What lordlike figure hit the Top Three with 'Please Don't Go'?

IT'S NOW OR NEVER

Listed below are song titles from the 80s. One word has been omitted from each title, all you have to do is find that one word.

1   'Thank You For The ......' – ABBA
2   '...... At The Lost And Found' – Meat Loaf
3   'The Gay ......' – Steve Wright
4   '...... Time' – Status Quo
5   'The Story Of The ......' – Wah!
6   'It's Raining ......' – Weather Girls
7   'Let's Hear It For The ......' – Deniece Williams
8   'Private ......' – Grace Jones
9   'The ...... Of Hissing Sid' – Keith Michell
10 '...... Mai' – Ennio Morricone

1   '...... Girl' – Rick Springfield
2   'Love ......' – Kim Wilde
3   'Love ......' – Belle and the Devotions
4   'The ...... Mouth' – Kajagoogoo
5   '...... In Motion' – JBs All Stars
6   'Killed By ......' – Motorhead
7   'Nobody's ......' – Haircut 100
8   '...... In The Air' – Don McLean
9   '...... Triangle' – Barry Manilow
10 '...... In The Wood' – Matchbox

1   '...... Romance' – Belle Stars
2   'Small Town ......' – Kane Gang
3   'Just A ......' – Nena
4   'What ......' – Orange Juice
5   'Girl ......' – Hot Chocolate
6   'Your ......' – Pluto Shervington
7   'Paris By ......' – Tygers Of Pan Tang
8   'Don't ......' – Hank Marvin
9   '...... Of Love' – Pretenders
10 '...... Of The World' – MFSB

THE OTHER SIDE OF LOVE

You can remember a lot of the number one hit singles in Britain, but can you remember what was on the other side of all those number ones? In this quiz, we list the titles of the B-sides of 60 number ones over the years, and all you have to do is name the A side and the artist. In order to be consistent, this quiz deals with the 7 inch version of each hit, not the 12 inch version, which in most cases has a different song on the B side, or at least a different mix from the smaller version.

1   'Careless Whisper Instrumental'
2   'Careless Talk'
3   'Freedom Instrumental'
4   'Feed The World'
5   'One September Monday'
6   'One February Friday'
7   'Make Me Smile (Come Up And See Me)'
8   'Wake Me Up Before You Go-go Instrumental'
9   'Grace' by Quincy Jones
10   'She's A Woman'
11   'Call Me (Instrumental)'
12   'Ich Bleib' Im Bett'
13   'Rock Your Baby Part Two'
14   'Where Did Our Love Go?'
15   'Hey Hey Helen'
16   'Yes It Is'
17   'Child Of The Moon'
18   'Thank You Girl'
19   'Misty Circles'
20   'It's All The Rage'

1   'Disco Down'
2   'Dubious'
3   'It/I Can't Stand It (demo)'
4   'Chinatown'
5   'Guitar Star'
6   'Die Young Stay Pretty'
7   'Woman'
8   'Suzy and Jeffrey'
9   'Street Thunder'
10   'Thank You, Mercy'
11   'Somewhere In The City'
12   'Melody Hill'
13   'Impossible Dream'
14   'Take Me Back'
15   'Genesis (In The Beginning)'
16   'Sufferin''
17   'Take You On A Saturday'
18   'Gamblin' Man'
19   'She Rowed'
20   'If Love Is Not The Reason'

1   'It's Too Hard To Say Goodbye'
2   'Give Love A Chance'
3   'Somewhere In My Life'
4   'To Turn You On'
5   'I Want To Make You Smile'
6   'It's Gonna Rain'
7   'Home'
8   'Little Kids'
9   'The You I Need'
10   'Knowin' She's There'

11	'Kid Dynamo'	16	'Watch Out'
12	'Window'	17	'Hello Misty Morning'
13	'Count Me Out'	18	'You Could Have Told Me'
14	'Till I Get It Right'	19	'Can't Keep My Mind On The Game'
15	'You've Got The Music Inside'	20	'Need A Lot Of Lovin''

QUIZ 48	COUNTDOWN TO ECSTASY

This quiz is similar to quiz number 14, except the titles are those of albums rather than singles. Again, scoring is reversed: three points for guessing the artist from the section A clue, two if from B, one if from C.

1	*Smiley Smile*	11	*Tanx*
2	*The Singles – The First Ten Years*	12	*Flogging A Dead Horse*
3	*Powerage*	13	*Kinda Latin*
4	*Dirk Wears White Socks*	14	*21 At 33*
5	*Rarities*	15	*Beat Crazy*
6	*Living Eyes*	16	*Foxtrot*
7	*Heaven And Hell*	17	*Here My Dear*
8	*Sandinista*	18	*The Basement Tapes*
9	*On The Border*	19	*Saucerful Of Secrets*
10	*Bayou Country*	20	*Coda*

1	*Holland*	12	*The Great Rock 'n' Roll Swindle*
2	*Voulez-Vous*	13	*I'm 21 Today*
3	*Highway to Hell*	14	*Tumbleweed Connection*
4	*Friend Or Foe*	15	*Jumpin' Jive*
5	*1967–70*	16	*The Lamb Lies Down On Broadway*
6	*Odessa*	17	*Midnight Love*
7	*Master Of Reality*	18	*Street Legal*
8	*Give 'Em Enough Rope*	19	*Atom Heart Mother*
9	*Desperado*	20	*In Through The Out Door*
10	*Willy And The Poor Boys*		
11	*The Slider*		

QUIZ 49	BEAUTY AND THE BEAST

Identify the following animal lovers:

1

2

3

4

5

Listed below are three tracks from well known or perhaps slightly less well known albums. All you have to do is to name the album and the artists involved.

1 'One Night In Bangkok', 'Heaven Help My Heart', 'I Know Him So Well'

2 'Two Tribes', 'Ferry Cross The Mersey', 'Born To Run'

3 'My Favourite Things', 'Edelweiss', 'Climb Ev'ry Mountain'

4 'Hello', 'All Night Long (All Night)', 'Stuck On You'

5 'Some Like It Hot', 'Get It On (Bang A Gong)', 'Tunnel Of Love'

6 'Things Can Only Get Better', 'Look Mama', 'Hunger For The Flesh'

7 'When I'm 64', 'Fixing A Hole', 'Lucy In The Sky With Diamonds'

8 'Starman', 'Hang On To Yourself', 'Rock'n'Roll Suicide'

9 'Radio Gaga', 'Keep Passing The Open Windows', 'Hammer To Fall'

10 'Your Love Is King', 'Cherry Pie', 'Why Can't We Live Together'

11 'Pretty Vacant', 'E.M.I.', 'God Save The Queen'

12 'Credit Card Baby', 'Heartbeat', 'Freedom'

13 'Wouldn't It Be Nice', 'God Only Knows', 'I Just Wasn't Made For These Times'

14 'Painter Man', 'Brown Girl In The Ring', 'Heart Of Gold'

15 'It's You', 'I Just Called To Say I Love You', 'Don't Drive Drunk'

16 'Gimme Shelter', 'You Can't Always Get What You Want', 'Love In Vain'

17 'Beat It', 'Billie Jean', Wanna Be Startin' Something'

18 'You Took The Words Right Out Of My Mouth', 'Two Out Of Three Ain't Bad', 'All Revved Up'

19 'Hungry Like The Wolf', 'Save A Prayer', 'New Religion'

20 'I Won't Let The Sun Go Down On Me', 'Shame On You', 'Wouldn't It Be Good'

1. 'I'm Not In Love', 'Life Is A Minestrone', 'Flying Junk'
2. 'Bite The Hand That Feeds', 'Everything Must Change', 'I Was In Chains'
3. 'Shout', 'Everybody Wants To Rule The World', 'I Believe'
4. 'More Than This', 'Take A Chance With Me', 'True To Life'
5. 'I Kissed The Spikey Fridge', 'Love And Pride', 'Fish'
6. 'Come Together', 'Here Comes The Sun', 'Mean Mr. Mustard'
7. 'Like Clockwork', 'She's So Modern', 'Me and Howard Hughes'
8. 'A Love In Vain', 'I Want To Know What Love Is', 'Tooth And Nail'
9. 'Automatic', 'Neutron Dance', 'Operator'
10. 'Cosmic Dancer', 'Get It On', 'Rip Off'
11. 'Getting So Excited', 'Total Eclipse Of The Heart', 'Take Me Back'
12. 'Flick Of The Wrist', 'Now I'm Here', 'Stone Cold Crazy'
13. 'Ocean Deep', 'Please Don't Fall In Love', 'Love Stealer'
14. 'Living For The City', 'Higher Ground', 'Jesus Children Of America'
15. 'The Winner Takes It All', 'On And On And On', 'Happy New Year'
16. 'Too Much Heaven', 'I'm Satisfied', 'Until'
17. 'Mother', 'King Of Pain', 'Tea In The Sahara'
18. 'Money', 'Time', 'The Great Gig In The Sky'
19. 'Fields Of Fire', '1000 Stars', 'The Storm'
20. 'Would I Lie To You', 'I Love You Like A Ball And Chain', 'Adrian'

1. 'Even Now', 'Shame On The Moon', 'Comin' Home'
2. 'Baba O'Riley', 'My Wife', 'Won't Get Fooled Again'
3. 'Only Love Can Break Your Heart', 'Southern Man', 'Crippled Creek Ferry'
4. 'Empty Garden', 'Legal Boys', 'All Quiet On The Western Front'
5. 'Romeo And Juliet', 'Les Boys', 'Tunnel Of Love'
6. 'The Headmaster Ritual', 'That Joke Isn't Funny Anymore', 'Nowhere Fast'
7. 'Madam Butterfly', 'Carmen', 'Lauretta'
8. '½ A Loaf', 'Just Another Night', 'Secrets'
9. 'To Have And To Have Not', 'A New England', 'The Man In The Iron Mask'

10 'Since I Don't Have You', 'Miss You Nights', 'Bright Eyes'
11 'A Boy Like Me A Girl Like You', 'Return To Sender', 'We're Coming In Loaded'
12 'Dancing With Mr. D', 'Angie', 'Star Star'
13 'America', 'Fakin' It', 'At The Zoo'
14 'Willie And The Hand Jive', 'I Shot The Sheriff', 'Mainline Florida'
15 'I Threw It All Away', 'Lay Lady Lay', 'Country Pie'
16 'Daniel', 'Elderberry Wine', 'Have Mercy On The Criminal'
17 'What's Happening Brother', 'God Is Love', 'Mercy Mercy Me (The Ecology)'
18 'Three Little Birds', 'Waiting In Vain', 'Jamming'
19 'Blue Moon Of Kentucky', 'Young And Beautiful', 'Milkcow Blues Boogie'
20 'Hard Headed Woman', 'Wild World', 'Longer Boats'

| QUIZ 51 | IT'S ALL IN THE GAME |

This is the spot for keep-fit fanatics, for those trying desperately to have a body like Mike Read's. All these questions have some connection, however loose, with the sporting life. Jockstraps should be worn while answering.

Who had the UK smashes with these titles?

1 'Chariots Of Fire'
2 'The Boxer'
3 'Eye Of The Tiger' (from the boxing movie *Rocky III*)
4 'Games People Play'
5 'The Winner Takes It All'
6 'Deck Of Cards' (two answers here)
7 'I'm Gonna Run Away From You'
8 'Walk Don't Run'
9 'Fly Robin Fly'
10 'The Game Of Love'
11 'Games Without Frontiers'
12 'Gamblin' Man'
13 'Gin House Blues'
14 '(Win Place Or Show) She's A Winner'

15 'Run Run Run'

16 'Run Runaway'

17 'Runaway'

18 'Physical'

19 'Jump'

20 'Leap Up And Down (Wave Your Knickers In The Air)'

Football songs – which team was the subject of each of these memorable musical moments?:

1 'Blue Is The Colour'

2 'We Can Do It'

3 'We've Got The Whole World In Our Hands'

4 'Nice One Cyril'

5 'Ossie's Dream'

6 'Easy Easy'

7 'Back Home'

8 'Ole Ola'

9 'We Have A Dream'

10 'Here We Go'

Now back to all sports:

11 Which song gave Cliff Richard his biggest US hit at that point in his career in 1963–4?

12 Which number one hit from 10 C.C. mentions cricket?

13 Who wrote a tribute to Geoff Boycott and John Snow entitled 'When An Old Cricketer Leaves The Crease'?

14 Who was under satirical attack from The Brat via the hit 'Chalk Dust – The Umpire Strikes Back'?

15 Which supergroup had a minor hit 'Anyone For Tennis'?

16 Which David Bowie smash might have been inspired by the England/Australia cricket Test Matches?

17 Which Blondie smash could be taken as a warning to swimmers?

18 Which world-famous boxer recorded the Ben E. King classic 'Stand By Me' as a single in 1964?

19 Which Abba biggie might have been mistaken for a sporting dictionary?

20 Who was the subject of Don Fardon's 1970 hit 'Belfast Boy'?

1 Which activity gave both Van Halen and the Pointer Sisters big 1984 hits that had extremely similar titles?

2 What is the sporting link between 'Gonna Fly Now' and 'Eye Of The Tiger'?

3 Who got Lifted in 1975 up to number 37 in the US charts, a year after his only other US Top 40 smash, which went all the way to number one in both Britain and America?

4 Which instrumental combo began their recording success in the US with a number which could have been about shooting entitled 'Crossfire'?

5 Which group with a long-distance name had an American Top 20 item entitled 'Peanut Butter'?

6 What was the Olympics' only British Top 20 hit?

7 Why were the Olympic Runners, who had four minor hits in 1978–9, so called?

8 What hit song did the Hot Shots revive with success in 1973?

9 Who warbled about 'The Boat That I Row' in the UK hit parade?

10 And who wrote the above hit?

11 What was the title of the other side of Queen's hit 'Fat Bottomed Girls' which was also credited as a hit title?

12 What sporting classic did the Mixtures bequeath us?

13 Who scraped into the UK Top 50 in 1978 with a song called 'The Race Is On'?

14 Which distinguished broadcaster and pianist had one chart hit, in 1963, entitled 'Pied Piper (The Beeje)'? His name provides the sporting link

15 Who had hits with 'Flying Machine', 'Hot Shot' and 'Shooting From The Heart'?

16 Who went to the 'Dogs' in 1968?

17 Who had a big US success with 'The Gambler'?

18 Which Englishman who had a Top Ten US hit in 1965 with 'You Turn Me On' which never made the UK charts at all, scored his first US chart rating with 'This Sporting Life'?

19 Which Elvis Presley movie (from 1966) featured our hero as a racing driver and provided him with a Top 40 hit in the US with the movie's title song?

20 Who had a gold single with 'The Main Event/Fight' in 1979?

QUIZ 52	IF I RULED THE WORLD

All questions in this quiz refer to royal names, either of artists or songs.

1 What was Queen's biggest British hit?
2 What is the name of Paul Young's backing group?
3 Who was KC and the Sunshine Band's royal night owl?
4 Name Roger Miller's Grammy-winning monarch
5 What was the regal side of U.B.40's first hit?
6 What real-life royals topped the album chart?
7 Who sang lead on the Drifters' 'Save The Last Dance For Me'?
8 What monarch was rhapsodized by Elvis Presley in 1958?
9 Adam and the Ants were monarchs of what domain?
10 Sting was sovereign of what realm?
11 What female royal did Queen imply was dangerous?
12 Who recorded 'Love And Pride'?
13 What monarch was the subject of an ABBA number one?
14 Who has charted under at least eight pseudonyms?
15 It was a shame she temporarily dropped her nickname
16 What colourful rulers held court in the Top Ten LP lists of late 1969?
17 What was Madness' first hit?
18 Whose album *Tapestry* was for a period the all-time best-selling LP?
19 Fifteen years after he sighed 'The Thrill Is Gone', this bluesman recorded the theme to the movie *Into the Night*
20 Who warned record buyers of the menace of Al Capone?

1 Who made the hit version of 'Louie Louie'?
2 Who took a chart dip in 'The River' in 1982?
3 Who wore 'Short Shorts'?
4 What was Tina Turner's recent royal rumination?
5 On what album did the Beatles include an untitled track about Her Majesty the Queen?
6 What was Killing Joke's follow-up to their 1985 hit 'Love Like Blood'?
7 What is Prince's real name?

8 Who ordered Bobby Darin to dance?

9 What deceased royal inspired comedian Steve Martin to burst into song?

10 The Hollies remembered which backward monarch?

11 What rhythm and blues greats recorded the LP *King and Queen*?

12 What thronesitter gave Generation X their biggest hit?

13 Who ruled the Average White Band?

14 Who was Chuck Berry's favourite royal?

15 Who was Gene Pitney's royal romance?

16 What song gave Dave Edmunds a British hit and Juice Newton an American winner?

17 'She Wears My Ring' gave what artist a Top Three hit in 1968?

18 By what name was saxophonist Curtis Ousley better known?

19 What royal lived in the boondocks?

20 What threesome reached the Top Five with 'Tom Dooley'?

1 What was Jody Miller's answer to 'King Of The Road'?

2 Who saluted the 'King Of The Cops'?

3 Who was Annette's fruity royal?

4 In what hit did Sammy Turner pledge that if he were king you would be queen?

5 What Australians found themselves 'Switched On Swing' in 1982?

6 Who reaped an American chart crop with 'Dancing In The Moonlight'?

7 Who went up Wolverton Mountain?

8 For how many weeks was Adam and the Ants' 'Prince Charming' number one?

9 Who saluted 'Her Royal Majesty'?

10 Who had their biggest British hit with 'A White Sport Coat'?

11 What monarch asked audiences to 'Groove Me'?

12 To whom did Neil Sedaka take a Top 30 bow in the spring of 1962?

13 Whose cover version of 'Memories Are Made Of This' reached the Top Five?

14 James Brown detested what monarch?

15 Who took a chart walk down the 'Royal Mile'?

16 What was Ronnie McDowell's US Top 20 lament when Elvis Presley died?

17 Who serenaded the 'Prince Of Darkness'?

18 Who got heavy with the 'Princess of the Night'?

19 Bill Haley's Comets recorded without Haley under what name?

20 Who paid musical tribute to the 'King Of Kings'?

QUIZ 53	IT TAKES TWO

This is an easy quiz to understand, if not quite so easy to find all the right answers. All the questions concern duos, some all male, some male and female, some all female and some not quite certain.

Complete the hitmaking duos:

1 Simon and

2 Soft

3 Tears For

4 Orchestral Manoeuvres

5 Daryl Hall and

6 Renee and

7 Chas and

8 Womack and

9 Ashford and

10 Captain and

11 Sonny and

12 Keith Harris and

13 Godley and

14 Grand Master and

15 Windsor Davies and

16 Michael Jackson and

17 Paul McCartney with

18 John Travolta and

19 Nina and

20 Ike and

Which duo hit with:

21 'Somethin' Stupid'

22 'Video Killed The Radio Star'

23 'Double Barrel'

24 'True Love'

25 'Don't Go Breakin' My Heart'

26 'Up Town Top Ranking'

27 'Sexcrime (nineteen eighty-four)'

28 'Cathy's Clown'

29 'Wake Me Up Before You Go Go'

30 'It's My Party'

31 'Only You'

32 'In The Year 2525'

33 'Islands In The Stream'

34 'A Rockin' Good Way'

35 'Agadoo'

36 'I Want To Hold Your Hand'

37 'I Know Him So Well'

38 'Yes Sir I Can Boogie'

39 'Together In Electric Dreams'

40 'Could It Be I'm Falling In Love'

Complete the hitmaking duos:

1 Peters and
2 Typically
3 Yarbrough and
4 Jet Harris and
5 David and
6 Jon and
7 Patience and
8 McFadden and
9 R and J
10 Santo and

11 Judy Clay and
12 Brian and
13 Jermaine Jackson and
14 Bell and
15 Pearl Carr and
16 Foster and
17 Lester Flatt and
18 Peter Cook and
19 Hugo and
20 England Dan and

Which duo hit with:

21 'Reunited'
22 'A World Without Love'
23 'I'm Your Puppet'
24 'One Step Further'
25 'Calling Occupants Of Interplanetary Craft'
26 'Passing Strangers'
27 'You Don't Have To Be A Baby To Cry'
28 'You Don't Send Me Flowers'
29 'Cinderella Rockefella'
30 'Goodness Gracious Me'
31 'Sorrow'
32 'Don't Forget To Remember'
33 'La Yenka'
34 'I've Been Drinking'
35 'Mad Eyed Screamer'
36 'Theme From "The Apartment"'
37 'Rosetta'
38 'The Mountain's High'
39 'Yesterday's Gone'
40 'With You I'm Born Again'

Who has had separate hits in duos with each of:

1 Sammy Davis Jr and Nancy Sinatra
2 Donna Summer and Barry Gibb
3 Tammi Terrell and Mary Wells
4 Jane Wyman and David Bowie
5 Maggie Bell and Frida
6 Peabo Bryson and Donny Hathaway
7 Frankie Laine and Johnnie Ray
8 Sheila Walsh and Phil Everly
9 Willie Nelson and Diana Ross
10 Charlie Byrd and Joao Gilberto

Which two duos each hit with the following songs:

11 'Deep Purple'
12 'Mockingbird'
13 'All I Have To Do Is Dream'
14 'You're The One That I Want'
15 'Vaya Con Dios'

Who is the uncredited duettist on:

16 Sam Cooke's 'Bring It On Home To Me'
17 Meat Loaf's 'Dead Ringer For Love'
18 Big Dee Irwin's 'Swinging On A Star'
19 Ray Charles' 'Hit The Road Jack'
20 James Ingram's 'Yah Mo B There'

Complete the hitmaking duos:

21 Bo Kirkland and
22 Mac and
23 De Etta Little and
24 Kenny Everett and
25 Amii Stewart and
26 Bob and
27 Marilyn McCoo and
28 Ping Ping and
29 Alfi and
30 Edward Byrnes and

Which duo hit with:

31 'Rock Bottom'
32 'Stumblin' In'
33 'Blue Guitar'
34 'Holy Joe'
35 'Hole In The Bucket'
36 'Duelling Banjos'
37 'Gonna Get Along Without Ya Now'
38 'Everlasting Love'
39 'Don't Bring Me Your Heartaches'
40 'Teach Me To Twist'

QUIZ 54	A CHANGE IS GONNA COME

This questionnaire deals with changes of name. As you surely know, many famous music personalities have ditched their original moniker to find fame and fortune under some other handle. When you see some of the names some stars started out with, this is not surprising. There again, there have been a few cases when the individual might have done better to have stuck with what his parents chose for him. None of the co-authors of this book has (yet) felt the need for a permanent alias.

Who are these people now better known as?:

1   Terence Nelhams
2   Richard Starkey
3   Harry Webb
4   Doris Kappelhoff
5   Stuart Goddard
6   Charles Aznavurjan
7   Charles Eugene Boone
8   David Jones
9   Paul Pond
10 Eric Clapp

11 John Henry Deutschendorf
12 David Albert Cook
13 Constance Franconero
14 Ronald Wycherly
15 Reg Dwight
16 Arnold Dorsey
17 Charles Hardin Holley
18 Lewis Brian Hopkins-Jones
19 Kenneth King
20 George O'Dowd

Which stars came into the world with the following names (or received them very soon after entering it)?:

1	Richard Sarstedt	11	Gary Webb
2	Yvette Marie Stevens	12	Elaine Bickerstaff
3	Brenda Mae Tarpley	13	Eric Hilliard Nelson
4	William Broad	14	James Marcus Smith
5	Robert Zimmerman	15	Robert T. Velline
6	Terence Perkins	16	Charles Westover
7	Thomas Hicks	17	Nicholas Bates
8	Norma Deloris Eggstrom	18	David Batt
9	Dino Crocetti	19	Gordon Sumner
10	Frederick Bulsara	20	Paul Hewson

The following surnames are the real last names of 20 acts known professionally only by a single name – supply the well-known forename in each case.

1	Leitch	11	Olson
2	Ciccone	12	Strohmeyer-Gartside
3	Adu	13	Small
4	Safka	14	Swofford
5	Dimucci	15	Rogers Nelson
6	Burt	16	Kerner
7	Papathanassiou	17	Paris
8	Wilcox	18	Garrity
9	Funicello	19	Marsden
10	Forte	20	Fuqua

QUIZ 55	BACK IN THE OLD COUNTRY

All the questions in this quiz refer to names or titles with America, USA or US in them.

1. Who recorded 'We Are The World'?
2. What was Bruce Springsteen's first number one album?
3. On what album did Don McLean's 'Vincent' appear?
4. In what song did Simon and Garfunkel count cars on the New Jersey turnpike?
5. How did the Clash describe their ennui?
6. Who originated 'Bend Me Shape Me'?
7. Elvis Presley was a red-blooded American
8. Name the Beach Boys' first hit?
9. What meal did Supertramp sing about?
10. What Mickey Newbury single was successfully covered by Elvis Presley?
11. Joan Armatrading got a phone call from where?
12. Chuck Berry and Linda Ronstadt both reached the US top forty with what Berry composition?
13. In what single from *There Goes Rhymin' Simon* did Paul Simon dream he was dying?

1. Who was Tom Petty's red, white and blue sweetheart?
2. In what year did David Essex chart with 'America'?
3. What Survivor flop became the title track of a smash compilation LP?
4. A Frenchman cooed 'I Love America'. What is his name?
5. What Jay and the Americans song was originally meant for the Drifters?
6. Which Grateful Dead album cover featured a rose?
7. What was the only hit single by the Nice?
8. In what US Top Ten hit from *The Jazz Singer* did Neil Diamond actually recite part of "The Pledge of Allegiance"?
9. What 1959 classic did Bobby Bare record under the name Bill Parsons?
10. According to a late 1960s progressive classic, where were the Steve Miller Band dwelling?
11. What was the Ritchie Family's next hit after 'The Best Disco in Town'?

12 What is the longest single ever to make the US Top Thirty?

13 Name the patriotic 1982 Pointer Sisters track that was a hit in the US but not the UK

1 About which anatomical parts did Billy Ocean sing in 1979?

2 What was Simple Minds' first hit on the Virgin label?

3 In 1980 the Nitty Gritty Dirt Band reached the US Top Twenty with what possibly nightmarish title?

4 Where did James Brown say he lived?

5 What was the title of Byron MacGregor's US Top Five narration?

6 What kind of males did Petula Clark prefer?

7 Ray Stevens wanted his nation to speak to him

8 What was Survivor's first US chart single?

9 What David Ackles album was produced by Bernie Taupin?

10 These were not the most popular females of Sister Sledge

11 What blues supergroup featuring Mike Bloomfield recorded *An American Music Band*?

12 What American national song has Ray Charles almost made his own?

13 Who had a US Top Five hit in 1940 with Irving Berlin's 'God Bless America'?

QUIZ 56	THE MAGNIFICENT SEVEN

What is the link?

1 A lady from a Paul Anka song

2 A 1982 Cure hit

3 Earth, Wind and Fire's planet

4 Duran Duran's keyboards player

5 The 1967 train tour to Rainbow City

6 Early 70s 'One Fine Morning' US hitmakers sounding like Sam the Sham's group

7 John of the Walker Brothers real name

8 **Which American vocalist would be the answer to the eighth question?**

<table>
<tr><td>QUIZ 57</td><td>O SUPERMAN</td></tr>
</table>

All these questions are in some way connected with words beginning with the letter O.

1 Who is the 'Big O'?
2 Who came back with 'Caribbean Queen'?
3 Whose number one hit 'I Pretend' stayed 36 weeks on the chart?
4 Who was the 'Long Haired Lover From Liverpool'?
5 Who hit with the 'Tubular Bells' album?
6 Who sang lead on 'Tie A Yellow Ribbon Round The Old Oak Tree', by Dawn?
7 Who was married to John Lennon?
8 Who had three number one hits, starting with 'Puppy Love'?
9 Who hit number one with 'Clair'?
10 Whose 'Eighth Day' was her first hit?
11 Who partners Daryl Hall?
12 Whose 1981 album was called *Architecture And Morality*?
13 Which Crickets hit did Mud take to number one?
14 What song gave Yazoo and the Flying Pickets their biggest hits?
15 What was won by 'I Just Called To Say I Love You', and 'Three Coins In The Fountain'?
16 Who travelled to the top with 'Use It Up And Wear It Out'?
17 What did Keith Harris sing with his large green bird?
18 What was the flip of Elvis Presley's chart-topper 'I Got Stung'?
19 Who said, 'Hands Up (Give Me Your Heart)'?
20 Which one hit wonders scored with 'Michelle'?

1 Whose biggest single hit has been 'Portsmouth'?
2 From which German village did the Children's Choir who sang 'The Happy Wanderer' come?
3 Who had the hit with 'Good Morning Starshine' from *Hair*?
4 Whose 'Manhattan Spiritual' was a bigger hit in America than in his native country?
5 Who scored two hits with Wild Willy Barrett?
6 Who claimed "There's No Stopping Us" in 1984?

7   Who took 'Ob-La-Di, Ob-La-Da' to number one?

8   What was Michael Jackson's biggest selling album before *Thriller*?

9   Fleetwood Mac have hit with two singles whose titles begin with 'Oh'. What are they?

10   What was Desmond Dekker's first hit?

11   Whose 'Passion Killer' gave them a first week of chart glory?

12   What was Ohio Express' only hit?

13   What was Marie Osmond's only solo hit?

14   Whose 'Love Train' reached number nine in 1973?

15   What was Sally Oldfield's one hit?

16   What is Dusty Springfield's real name?

17   Who backed Mike Berry, and had two minor hits on their own?

18   What was MGM's final number one single in Britain?

19   And what was Roy Orbison's final number one single in Britain?

20   Which version of 'Oh No Not My Baby' climbed higher in the charts, Rod Stewart's or Manfred Mann's?

1   Who danced the body music?

2   Who had three weeks on the singles chart, over a period of 12 years?

3   Who hit number one in America with 'Undercover Angel'?

4   Whose show featured Marie Adams?

5   Whose 'Lawnchairs' crept into the lower reaches of the charts in 1981?

6   How many weeks did Eddie Calvert's 'Oh Mein Papa' spend at number one?

7   What was Jonathan King's alias for the hit 'It Only Takes A Minute'?

8   Who managed the Rolling Stones at the time of their first hits?

9   Of which group was Sonny Til the lead singer?

10   Who sang lead on the Shirelles' 'Will You Love Me Tomorrow'?

11   Whose backing group is called The Buckaroos?

12   The Olympics hit with 'I Wish I Could Shimmy Like My Sister Kate'. Who recorded 'I Wish I Could Shimmy Like My Sister Arthur'?

13 Who was 'The Merry Ploughboy' for two weeks in 1966?

14 Which vocalist scored with two different backing groups, One Way and the Partners?

15 Whose 'Wah-Watusi' flopped in Britain, despite reaching the Top Ten in America?

16 What did Norman Petty, Sam Phillips and Chet Atkins fail to do, that Fred Foster succeeded with?

17 Which harpist took her album *Tranquillity* to number 12 early in 1980?

18 What made Donny and Marie Osmond's hit 'Morning Side Of The Mountain' different from their other three British hit singles?

19 Which hit single title starts 'Oh Oh'?

20 Who "called my baby on the telephone/To tell her half of my head was gone"?

QUIZ 58 | ON BROADWAY

A three-parter related to records and performers linked to the world of board-treading and first-night parties

From what show did the following songs come and who had the biggest UK hit record with each song?

1 'Oh What A Circus'

2 'I Don't Know How To Love Him'

3 'You'll Never Walk Alone'

4 'One Night In Bangkok'

5 'And I'm Telling You I'm Not Going'

6 'Take That Look Off Your Face'

7 'Maria'

8 'Aquarius'

9 'Rose Marie'

10 'I Know Him So Well'

11 'America'

12 'March Of The Siamese Children'

13 'Tell Me On A Sunday'

14 'I'll Put You Together Again'

15 'I Could Easily Fall'

16 'I Am What I Am'

17 'Big Spender'

18 'Climb Ev'ry Mountain'

19 'Any Dream Will Do'

20 'Pie Jesu'

1 Which American singer had a Top 40 US hit with 'Memory', from *Cats*?

2 And which two singers have hit the UK charts with 'Memory'?

3 Which singer who enjoyed 60s chart fame with 'First Cut Is The Deepest' appeared in the 1984 smash musical 'Starlight Express'?

4 And which singer from which male/female soul group also played in that show?

5 What Andrew Lloyd Webber composition other than 'Pie Jesu' took Latin into the Top Three?

6 Which West End show featured David Essex in his first leading London stage role?

7 Which artist was nearly 68 when he had his only UK number one hit single with a double-sided hit, one side of which was a song from *Cabaret*?

8 And what was the big single the same artist had from another successful stage musical four years earlier?

9 Who starred in the London stage show of *Fiddler On The Roof* and enjoyed a Top Ten hit with one of the songs from the show in 1967?

10 And what was the title of that song?

11 Who with two Top Ten hits in 1976 starred on the London stage in *Hair, Jesus Christ Superstar, Cats* and *Blondel*?

12 Which Broadway cast album first hit the UK charts in 1958 and eventually totalled a record-holding 129 weeks on the album lists, more than any other stage cast album?

13 Who followed up a big hit from what was to become a West End production with an Alice Cooper song?

14 And name the Alice Cooper number in question

15 Which album of a theatrical score featured both ex-Manfred Mann lead singers, Paul Jones and Mike d'Abo?

16 Who wrote *West Side Story* which, among many other achievements, gave P. J. Proby two massive single hits?

17 What was the title of the instrumental album by Andrew Lloyd Webber that became the basis of the second half of one of his West End hits?

18 And who was the featured soloist on the album?

19 The Jackson Five had a US Top 20 hit in 1972 with 'Corner Of The Sky'. From which Broadway hit show did this come?

20 What was the main difference between the two chart-topping duets from *Grease* – 'You're The One That I Want' and 'Summer Nights'?

In each of the following lists of songs, one of the number is not from the same stage show as the others. Identify the odd one out and name the majority's show.

1 'Easy To Be Hard', 'Frank Mills', 'Good Morning Starshine', 'People'

2 'Climb Ev'ry Mountain', 'Happy Talk', 'My Favourite Things', 'Edelweiss'

3 'Tonight', 'Maria', 'On The Street Where You Live', 'Somewhere'

4 'Don't Cry For Me Argentina', 'Memory', 'Another Suitcase In Another Hall', 'I'd Be Surprisingly Good For You'

5 'On The Street Where You Live', 'What I Did For Love', 'Nothing', 'One'

Which record hit of a song from a stage show described the following:
(Title, artist and show all required)

6 The attractiveness of a small white plant

7 The attractions of the capital of Thailand

8 Our entry into a new constellation coupled with a request for more solar energy

9 A demand for circus entertainers

10 A request for a weekend news item

11 Cheerful conversation

12 Being lost in heavenly surroundings

13 The thoroughfare containing a loved one's abode

14 A request to approximately 30,000,000 people to keep stiff upper lips

And finally:

15 No less than four singers had Top 20 hits with one song from the musical *Pyjama Game* in 1955. Two were ladies, two gentlemen, all but one lady American. Name all four.

16 And what was that song that hit four times?

17 From what show did Matt Monro's 1961 hit 'Gonna Build A Mountain' come?

18 And who starred in and co-wrote the show just a short while after scoring two number one UK hits which he did not write?

19 What musical was a huge international hit for the author of pop number ones 'Living Doll' and 'Do You Mind'?

20 What was the hit song from the long-running *Rocky Horror Show*?

We associate special memories with particular songs. Do we associate years with certain artists? In this quiz we ask you to identify the best year of the named act. By ''best'' we mean that year in which they scored their most number ones or, if no number ones, most Top Ten hits. If the act never had a Top Ten hit, in what year did they have most chart entries? If there is a tie between years with the same tally of number ones, move on to Top Ten hits to decide; if a tie in Top Tenners, move to chart entries. Singles, not albums, should be counted for the purposes of this quiz.

1	Frankie Goes To Hollywood	11	Scott McKenzie
2	Michael Jackson	12	Kajagoogoo
3	Police	13	Roy Orbison
4	Gerry and the Pacemakers	14	Adam and the Ants
5	Bruce Springsteen	15	Bob Dylan
6	Beatles	16	ABBA
7	Dave Clark Five	17	Bobby Darin
8	Rolling Stones	18	Wham
9	Spandau Ballet	19	Slade
10	Bee Gees	20	Cliff Richard

1	Sex Pistols	11	Julio Iglesias
2	Shakin' Stevens	12	Harry Belafonte
3	Elvis Presley	13	Ultravox
4	Bill Haley and His Comets	14	Righteous Brothers
5	Jerry Lee Lewis	15	Del Shannon
6	Supremes	16	Madness
7	Elton John	17	Partridge Family
8	Rod Stewart	18	Don McLean
9	Adam Faith	19	Donny Osmond
10	Frankie Laine	20	Cilla Black

1 Perry Como	12 M
2 Chuck Berry	13 Helen Reddy
3 Fleetwood Mac	14 Rainbow
4 Eagles	15 Jonathan Richman and the Modern Lovers
5 Shirley Bassey	
6 Frank Ifield	16 Doris Day
7 Odyssey	17 Spencer Davis Group
8 Frank Sinatra	18 Bucks Fizz
9 Brenda Lee	19 Al Green
10 Ramones	20 Santa Claus and the Christmas Trees
11 Dawn	

QUIZ 60 | MONEY MONEY MONEY

Every question in this quiz deals with riches. "Spend" some time answering these:

1 Who went to number one with 'Silver Lady'?

2 What was the Beatles' cheapest hit?

3 Who recorded 'Who Were You With In The Moonlight'?

4 Barrett Strong had a million seller with what Berry Gordy song?

5 Who reached the Top Three in 1975 with 'Money Honey'?

6 What was Spandau Ballet's precious metal?

7 Who sang 'Gonna Make You An Offer You Can't Refuse'?

8 What was Freda Payne's only number one?

9 What David Bowie album title mentions a precious stone?

10 Who hit the Top 20 with two different versions of 'Feel The Need In Me'?

11 What was 10 C.C.'s stock dance?

12 What was Shirley Bassey's precious digit?

13 Who had a number one called 'Diamonds'?

14 Who sang 'A Boy Named Sue'?

15 What bankrobbers were rhapsodized by Georgie Fame?

16 What pianist briefly teamed with Georgie Fame?

17 What Beatles' song named something money could not purchase?

18 Who reached the Top Five in 1977 with 'I Will'?

19 What was the Four Seasons' valuable badge?

20 Who successfully revived 'Money' in 1979?

1　For what were the Skids toiling?

2　The title of Gary 'U.S.' Bonds' biggest hit mentioned what American coin?

3　To whom did the Chairmen of the Board give money?

4　What was Dennis Brown's asset?

5　What thief did the Clash immortalize?

6　'Money Honey', a different song from that mentioned in section A, question 5, was recorded by Elvis Presley. Who originated the number?

7　What precious metal gave John Stewart his comeback hit?

8　What was Roy Orbison's last hit?

9　Where did Olivia Newton-John deposit her royalties?

10　The Members ran what variety of financial service?

11　Billy Joel included a song about cash on *An Innocent Man*. What was it?

12　What was Ray Charles' expression for being broke?

13　What kind of grin did the Boomtown Rats offer?

14　The most valuable label of the 70s released Shirley and Company's 'Shame Shame Shame'. What was the company?

15　What did Shalamar advise doing with windfalls?

16　Who is remembered for 'The Birds And The Bees'?

17　How did an agent pay Buffalo Springfield?

18　One of the favourite songs of the artist referred to in section A, question 16 was 'Where Were You (On Our Wedding Day)?' Who was the American singer?

19　What Beatles classic got its name from a Julian Lennon remark?

20　What was Steve Miller's attitude to wealth?

1　The Upsetters made the Top Five with 'Return Of Django'. The other side was also listed on the chart. What was it?

2　What financial calamity did Gene Pitney foresee?

3　The J. Geils Band covered what Contours piece?

4　According to Elton John, what could mother not provide?

5　According to James Brown, what effect will money have on you?

6　Where did the Skyliners get their coins?

7　Who scored in 1980 with 'A Lover's Holiday'?

8　What singer had the US hit of 'For The Good Times'?

9 The Four Preps reached the Top Forty with what medley?

10 How did Kenny Ball satisfy his Jazzmen?

11 Who recorded the dance sensation 'Twine Time'?

12 What bill did the Kingston Trio possess?

13 What were the Springfields' valuable assets?

14 Who went to the Top Ten in 1968 with 'Everything I Am'?

15 What financial wisdom did Al Kent offer?

16 What monetary situation thrilled George Jones and Gene Pitney?

17 Who recorded 'Two-Bit Manchild'?

18 How did James Brown satisfy his creditors?

19 Who popularized 'The Stroll'?

20 What did the Rolling Stones like to spend?

| QUIZ 61 | NINETEEN EIGHTY-FOUR |

Just how much do you remember of the very recent past? All questions refer to records and/or incidents of 1984.

Who had these hits:

1 'Apollo 9'

2 'Nobody Told Me'

3 'Footloose'

4 'She Bop'

5 'Madam Butterfly'

6 'One Love/People Get Ready'

7 'Love Me Tender'

8 'Ocean Deep/Baby You're Dynamite'

9 'A Rockin' Good Way'

10 'Listen To Your Father'

11 'Heaven Knows I'm Miserable Now'

12 'William It Was Really Nothing'

13 'Swimming Horses'

14 'Hand In Glove'

15 'Cherry Oh Baby'

16 'Passengers'

17 'Hammer To Fall'
18 'Susanna'
19 'Can't Buy Me Love'
20 '(Wood Beez) Pray Like Aretha Franklin'

And these lesser (on the whole) smashes:

1   'Give Me More Time'
2   'Up On The Catwalk'
3   'Emergency (Dial 999)'
4   '99$\frac{1}{2}$'
5   'High On Emotion'
6   'The Greatness and Perfection Of Love'
7   'The Judgement Is The Mirror'
8   'You're Never Too Young'
9   'Hotline To Heaven'
10 'The Chant Has Just Begun'

Who had hits with these albums:

11 *Mange Tout*
12 *The Fish People Tapes*
13 *Lament*
14 *Now That's What I Call Music*
15 *Points On The Curve*
16 *Would Ya Like More Scratchin'?*
17 *Breaking Hearts*
18 *Sisters*
19 *1984*
20 *1984 (for the love of Big Brother)*

1 Which American act made a chart comeback towards the end of the year with a record made in Italy?

2 Two singles from the album *Chess* were released at the end of 1984. One, 'One Night In Bangkok' was a hit. The other was not. Name it

3 Who are Terry, Karl and Toby?

4 Who was the Ivor Novello Songwriter of the Year in 1984?

5 Which two female artists recorded albums of famous movie songs in 1984? (Both charted)

6 For how many weeks was Frankie Goes To Hollywood's debut album top of the album charts?

7 Who starred in the West End musical *Little Me* and hit the charts with what turned out to be his first Top Ten hit at the very end of the year?

8 Whose number was 54–46?

9 What label are Everything But The Girl on?

10 Which act, returning to the single charts for the first time in 16 years, toured Britain with great success?

11 How many hit singles emerged from the musical *Starlight Express* in 1984?

12 And which trio lost one of its members to that show?

13 What was the most obvious difference in the label information of 'Careless Whisper' as far as the US and UK releases were concerned?

14 Who had a chart album entitled *Girls Just Wanna Have Fun*?

15 Who dedicated a hit to "the original spirit of the Olympic Games"?

16 What was the title of Prince's only number one UK hit in 1984?

17 Who played guitar on 'Teardrops'?

18 Why was Germany big in Japan?

19 Who had "two strong arms, blessings of Babylon"?

20 What link was established between Alvin Stardust and the Kursaal Flyers in 1984?

QUIZ 62	THE SINGER SANG HIS SONG

For this quiz you will have to flick back through the pages and look at the titles of the previous quizzes. Try to name the artists *most* associated with the songs used as the titles, and award yourself one point for each correct answer.

QUIZ 1 **WHERE ARE YOU NOW (MY LOVE)**

	A		B		C
1	Hollywood	1	London	1	Sunny Goodge St.
2	Bangkok	2	Eton	2	Zululand
3	Japan	3	Africa	3	Bethlehem
4	The World	4	Down Under (Australia)	4	Thika
5	The World	5	Moon	5	Nairobi
6	China	6	Sun	6	Colorado
7	New York	7	Daytona	7	Nassau
8	The Moon	8	Lebanon	8	Georgia
9	Argentina	9	San Damiano	9	King's Road
10	Mersey	10	London	10	Nile
11	Hersham	11	Bangor	11	59th Street Bridge
12	Caribbean	12	Zambesi	12	Fort Worth
13	Vienna	13	Croydon	13	Galveston
14	Moscow	14	Indiana	14	Jarrow
15	Manchester	15	Kentucky	15	El Paso
16	Amsterdam	16	Siam	16	Pasadena
17	Paris (Young Parisians)	17	Winchester	17	Georgia
18	California	18	New Orleans	18	Irish Sea
19	In America	19	Dublin	19	Montego Bay
20	The USA	20	Wembley	20	Alaska

QUIZ 2 **A LITTLE BIT OF SOAP**

1 Peter Noone (Herman's Hermits)
2 Paul McCartney
3 Dynasty
4 Dallas Boys
5 Chris Sandford and 'Not Too Little, Not Too Much'
6 Davy Jones of the Monkees
7 'Love Me Tender'
8 Priscilla, the wife of the late singer, stars in the serial
9 They've all had Top Ten hits with songs featured in *Crossroads*
10 John Leyton with 'Johnny Remember Me'

ANSWERS

QUIZ 3 LIVING IN THE PAST

1	Big Bopper	11	Ricky Nelson
2	Buddy Holly	12	Bobby Darin
3	Marty Wilde	13	Cliff Richard
4	Jane Morgan	14	Craig Douglas
5	Platters	15	Anthony Newley
6	Everly Brothers	16	Emile Ford and The Checkmates
7	Elvis Presley	17	Adam Faith
8	Elvis Presley	18	Frank Sinatra
9	Russ Conway	19	Johnny and The Hurricanes
10	Shirley Bassey	20	Frankie Laine

1   Conway Twitty (the standard was 'Mona Lisa')
2   The deaths of Buddy Holly, Ritchie Valens and The Big Bopper in a plane crash
3   Lord Rockingham's XI (Benny Green on tenor – 'Hoots Mon' their biggie and 'Wee Tom' the other)
4   Russ Conway
5   Johnny and The Hurricanes
6   Shirley Bassey
7   'As I Love You'
8   Johnny Horton
9   Ruby Murray
10 Bobby Darin (with 'Mack The Knife')
11 He is Russ Conway, the year's most charted act in the UK
12 He is Craig Douglas who hit the top with 'Only Sixteen'
13 He recorded the original version of 'Only Sixteen' (which he co-wrote) but Craig Douglas had the British hit
14 Anthony Newley (with 'I've Waited So Long' and the *Idle On Parade* EP)
15 Jerry Keller, with a number one hit 'Here Comes Summer' in the autumn
16 Paul Anka
17 Duane Eddy
18 His version was a cover of the original by Phil Phillips – Phillips' version was not big in the UK
19 Wink Martindale, as revealed in his 'Deck Of Cards'
20 'Baby Face'

1   He had a hit entitled 'Waterloo', as did ABBA in 1974 with a different song
2   Neil Sedaka
3   He had a hit (US only) with 'Tragedy', as did the Bee Gees in 1979 with a different song
4   'Makin' Love' by Floyd Robinson
5   Annette
6   Cyril Stapleton
7   Billy Eckstine ('Gigi')
8   He did not go into the recording studio during 1959
9   It was number one album in the UK all year
10 Eddie Hodges

11 'A Pub With No Beer'
12 *77 Sunset Strip*
13 Pat Boone (he also had a hit record with the same title)
14 Fabian
15 'Why'
16 Henry Mancini
17 Dave "Baby" Cortez
18 Playmates
19 'My Heart Is An Open Book' although his only UK chart record was the minor 1960 hit 'Lucky Devil'
20 The Frantic Five

QUIZ 4 C'MON AND SWIM

1 Gerry and the Pacemakers (also acceptable: Frankie Goes To Hollywood)
2 Nile Rodgers
3 Greg Lake
4 Deep Purple
5 Lobo
6 'Oliver's Army'
7 Elkie Brooks
8 Rod Stewart
9 'Seven Seas Of Rhye'
10 Billy Ocean
11 Ike Turner
12 Paul McCartney
13 'Rivers Of Babylon'
14 'Green River'
15 'Sea Of Love'
16 1970
17 'Water On Glass'
18 Supremes
19 Danny Williams
20 *The River*

1 'Beyond The Sea'
2 *Blue Moves*
3 Johnny Rivers
4 'Water Water'
5 'Watching The River Flow'
6 Osmonds
7 'Red River Rock'
8 'Black Water'
9 Al Hudson
10 'Ain't No Mountain High Enough'
11 'Julie Ocean'
12 Brook Benton
13 Band
14 Jimmy Cliff
15 'Boat On The River'
16 Brenda Lee
17 Hudson-Ford
18 *The Poseidon Adventure* ('The Morning After')
19 Bobby Darin
20 Pussycat

1 Ramsey Lewis Trio
2 Muddy Waters
3 Atlantic
4 'Indian Lake'
5 Blind Faith
6 Brook Brothers
7 Gladys Knight and the Pips
8 'Dirty Water'
9 Don Gibson
10 'Moody River'
11 'The River'
12 Danny Rivers
13 'Drowning In A Sea Of Love'
14 Godiego or Peter MacJunior
15 Norman Brooks
16 Patti Page
17 'The Water Is Over My Head'
18 'Down By The River'
19 Johnnie and Joe
20 John Leyton

ANSWERS

QUIZ 5 YOU'RE MORE THAN A NUMBER IN MY LITTLE RED BOOK

1	20th	11	Seven
2	96	12	Five
3	48	13	5-4-3-2-1
4	1000	14	One
5	1999	15	68
6	9	16	Nine
7	Number Nine	17	9 to 5
8	Second	18	67
9	747	19	15
10	69	20	Number 1

1	13th	11	1964
2	Six	12	One
3	Two	13	Three
4	Millions	14	Four
5	17	15	Seven
6	2000	16	3×3
7	Four	17	Two
8	20th	18	1000
9	5:15	19	1963
10	Three	20	100

1	23	11	Number 9
2	Five	12	One
3	One	13	1962
4	Thousands	14	1980
5	60s	15	59th
6	2525	16	999
7	3rd	17	Second
8	101	18	18
9	14–18	19	25 or 6 to 4
10	Four	20	Four

QUIZ 6   PEOPLE ARE PEOPLE

1	Simon	11	'Woman In Love'
2	Osmond	12	'Forever and Ever'
3	Harris	13	'Young Love'
4	Robinson	14	'This Ole House'
5	Smith	15	'Cherry Pink and Apple Blossom White'
6	Starr	16	'Mary's Boy Child'
7	Stevens	17	'Only You'
8	Stewart	18	'My Way'
9	Williams	19	'This Is My Song'
10	Young	20	'Fire'

1	Berry	11	'Think'
2	James	12	'Tell Him'
3	Baker	13	'Mack The Knife'
4	Taylor	14	'Tonight'
5	Wilson	15	'Heartbreak Hotel'
6	Barry	16	'Iko Iko'
7	Thomas	17	'The Lion Sleeps Tonight'
8	Brown	18	'Let Me Go Lover'
9	Bennett	19	'Lucille'
10	Williams	20	'Why'

1	Charles	11	'Mama'
2	Hawkins	12	'My Girl'
3	Jackson	13	'Paper Roses'
4	Lee	14	'Save Me'
5	Miller	15	'She's Not There'
6	Ruffin	16	'Star'
7	Nelson	17	'Stand By Me'
8	McLean (not Everly!)	18	'It's The Same Old Song'
9	Jones	19	'Indian Love Call'
10	Scott	20	'Hot Love'

ANSWERS

QUIZ 7 SWEDISH RHAPSODY

1 The letters each stand for a first name of a group member – Agnetha, Björn, Benny, Anni-Frid (Frida)
2 Agnetha Fältskog, Björn Ulvaeus, Benny Andersson, Anni-Frid (Frida) Lyngstad. All spellings, including "ss" in Andersson, and all accents must be correct!
3 'Waterloo'
4 Eurovision Song Contest 1974
5 Elvis Presley, Cliff Richard and Beatles
6 Epic
7 'Money Money Money'
8 'Take A Chance On Me'
9 Björn and Benny
10 Benny
11 Stockholm
12 Björn
13 Björn
14 A large spotlight
15 *Chess*
16 Their name is spelled the same way backwards as forwards – a word or sentence with this property is a palindrome
17 A mnemonic is an aid to memory, often provided by initials – the group name reminds one of the individual names in this way
18 The two-man two-girl group Brotherhood Of Man
19 'Money Money Money' and 'Gimme Gimme Gimme', though the latter was followed by 'A Man After Midnight' in parentheses
20 Frida

1 'Dancing Queen'
2 Stig Anderson (one "s")
3 'The Day Before You Came'
4 'I Know Him So Well'
5 Elaine Paige and Barbara Dickson
6 Polar
7 Phil Collins
8 Mike Chapman
9 Australia
10 UNICEF
11 'The Day Before You Came'
12 'Super Trouper'
13 Sweet Dreams
14 'Voulez Vous'/'Angel Eyes'
15 'Does Your Mother Know'
16 'I Do, I Do, I Do, I Do, I Do'
17 'The Girl With The Golden Hair'
18 'Thank You For The Music'
19 He produced Agnetha's second solo album
20 A run of consecutive Top Ten hits

ANSWERS

1 Michael B. Tretow
2 'Ring Ring'
3 Neil Sedaka and Phil Cody
4 'Elaine' (Paige)
5 'Ring Ring'
6 'Slowly'
7 Benny – The Hep Stars; Björn – The Hootenanny Singers
8 *Jesus Christ Superstar*
9 Olivia Newton-John: 'Long Live Love'
10 Australia
11 Both have hit the UK charts with a song entitled 'The Heat Is On'
12 Stonewall Jackson: 'Waterloo'
13 'Fernando'
14 He plays guitar
15 It is the title of the Spanish version of 'Knowing Me Knowing You'
16 'Pick A Bale Of Cotton', 'On Top Of Old Smokey' and 'Midnight Special'
17 'Why Did It Have To Be Me'
18 'Take A Chance On Me'
19 Atlantic
20 25

QUIZ 8 **A BEATLE I WANT TO BE**

1 Dora Bryan
2 The Rutles – a group created for a TV parody of the Beatles
3 'I Dig A Pony'
4 They all made their debut on the Beatles' Apple label
5 Bert Kaempfert
6 'Hey Jude'
7 John Lennon and Paul McCartney
8 They all had hits with George Harrison songs
9 *How I Won The War*
10 Paul

1 Brian Poole and the Tremeloes
2 Sonny Curtis of the Crickets
3 George Harrison produced Bangla Desh concert in which a galaxy of stars appeared including George and Ringo Starr
4 Jimmy Nicol – Shubdubs
5 'Cry For A Shadow'
6 'Love Me Do' (number 17) and 'Something/Come Together' (number four)
7 Climbing up the Eiffel Tower (from the song 'I Am The Walrus')
8 Astrid Kirchherr
9 *Yellow Submarine*
10 'Yesterday'

ANSWERS

1. John was Thisbe
   Paul was Pyramus
   George was Moonshine
   Ringo was Lion
2. 'Up Against It'
3. The Beatles and Gerry and the Pacemakers who together made a one-off appearance under that name on 19 October 1961 at Litherland Town Hall, Liverpool
4. (4 year old) Julian Lennon
5. 'Savoy Truffle'
6. George Harrison-'Wonderwall'
7. Apollo C. Vermooth
8. 'Sexy Sadie'
9. 'Tomorrow Never Knows'
10. Rory Storm and the Hurricanes

QUIZ 9 **THE BOSS**

1. E Street Band
2. 'Because The Night'
3. 'Dancing In The Dark'
4. 'Born To Run'
5. Pointer Sisters
6. *Darkness at the Edge of Town*
7. Big Daddy
8. Asbury Park
9. Little Steven and the Disciples of Soul
10. Manfred Mann's Earth Band
11. Clarence Clemmons
12. Gary "US" Bonds
13. *Born to Run*
14. *Nebraska*
15. 'We Are The World' by USA For Africa

1. John Hammond
2. Jon Landau
3. 'Hungry Heart'
4. 'Johnny Bye-Bye'
5. Brian de Palma
6. Dave Marsh
7. 'Sandy'
8. 'The River'
9. 'Rosalita'
10. Hammersmith Odeon
11. 'Spirit In The Night'
12. *Mask*
13. 'Trapped'
14. *The River*
15. 'Twist And Shout'

ANSWERS

1 *In Harmony 2*
2 John Sayles
3 Hollies
4 *No Nukes*
5 Annie Liebovitz
6 George Theiss
7 'Growing Up'
8 *The Real Paper*
9 'Hungry Heart'
10 'Cadillac Ranch'
11 'A Love So Fine'
12 Andy Pratt, 'Avenging Annie'
13 'Stay' (on *No Nukes*)
14 The writing is in script
15 Artie Shaw

QUIZ 10   **WEATHER FORECAST**

1 'Rainy Day Women Numbers 12 and 35'
2 'Rainin' In My Heart'
3 'Rain And Tears'
4 'Raindrops Keep Falling On My Head'
5 'Rain Forest'
6 'Rain Rain Rain'
7 'Rainy Night In Georgia'
8 'I Can't Stand The Rain'
9 'Walkin' In The Rain'
10 'I Wish It Would Rain'

1 'Sun Of Jamaica'
2 'Sunny Honey Girl'
3 'Sunshine Day'
4 'Sunshine Of Your Love'
5 'Sunshine After The Rain'
6 'I Won't Let The Sun Go Down On Me'
7 'Paper Sun'
8 'Ice In The Sun'
9 'I Live For The Sun'
10 'Hot Stuff'

QUIZ 11   **SPOT THE PIGEON**

1 Beatles
2 Adam and the Ants
3 Monkees
4 Echo and the Bunnymen
5 Kevin the Gerbil
6 Crickets
7 Boomtown Rats
8 A Flock Of Seagulls
9 Frog Chorus
10 Animals

11 'Teddy Bear'
12 'Baa Baa Black Sheep'
13 'The Lion Sleeps Tonight'
14 'Karma Chameleon'
15 Doves
16 'The Birdie Song (Birdie Dance)'
17 Love Cats
18 Snake
19 Rabbit
20 Nightingale

ANSWERS

1 Malcolm McLaren (Duck, Oyster, Buffalo and Butterfly!)
2 Budgie
3 Crazy Elephant
4 Butterfly
5 Thorn Birds
6 Marty Wilde
7 Lobo
8 Clyde
9 'Fox On The Run'
10 Piranhas
11 'Little Red Rooster'
12 Norma Tanega
13 America
14 'Wooly Bully', by Sam the Sham and the Pharoahs
15 'Nellie The Elephant'
16 That Doggie in the Window
17 Scorpions
18 'Spiders And Snakes'
19 Dog – 'Hot Dog' for Shaky and 'I Love My Dog' for Cat
20 A White Swan

1 Camel
2 Randy Newman
3 J. P. Richardson, the Big Bopper
4 Monkey
5 Horses
6 Boll Weevil
7 'Jet' and 'Martha My Dear'
8 A bird dog
9 Fox. 'S-s-single Bed' was by Fox, 'Mockingbird' by Inez and Charlie Foxx and 'Burning Car' by John Foxx
10 Crocodile. 'Crocodile Rock' by Elton John reached number five, while 'See You Later, Alligator' by Bill Haley peaked at number seven
11 'The Honeysuckle And The Bee' from Winifred Atwell's medley 'Let's Have Another Party'. Half marks only for B. Bumble, as a B. Bumble isn't an insect, though a bumble bee is
12 Muskrat
13 Robins
14 Dogs
15 'Nashville Cats'
16 Commodores
17 'Old Shep'
18 'The Birds and The Bees'
19 Yellow Dog
20 'D.I.V.O.R.C.E.'

QUIZ 12 ENGLAND SWINGS

1 Kinks
2 Ralph McTell
3 Roger Miller
4 Clash
5 New Vaudeville Band
6 Scaffold
7 New Vaudeville Band
8 Beatles
9 Alan Price
10 Simon and Garfunkel
11 Sham 69
12 Clash
13 Gerry Rafferty
14 Manchester Utd FC
15 Andy Stewart
16 Jimmie Rodgers
17 England World Cup Squad (the 1982 lot)
18 Boney M (But see Section C, Question 1)
19 Kirsty MacColl
20 Wings (Paul McCartney is not a correct answer)

1 Vera Lynn
2 Des O'Connor
3 Roger Whittaker
4 T. Rex
5 Dave Dee, Dozy, Beaky, Mick and Tich
6 Clash
7 Cockney Rejects
8 Don Fardon
9 Wings OR Light Of The World
10 Kinks
11 Wigan's Chosen Few and Wigan's Ovation
12 Acker Bilk ('White Cliffs Of Dover')
13 'Summer Set'
14 Billy Bragg
15 Roxy Music
16 Genesis
17 Motorhead
18 Hatfield And The North
19 Bangor
20 Reading

1 Barnbrack
2 Frank Sinatra
3 Booker T and the MGs
4 Marianne Faithfull
5 Liverpool Express
6 New Vaudeville Band
7 'Good Old Arsenal'
8 Raphael Ravenscroft
9 Lindisfarne
10 Electric Light Orchestra
11 Rose Garden
12 Glasgow
13 Glasgow
14 Bee Gees
15 Laurie London ('He's Got The Whole World In His Hands')
16 'Streets Of London'
17 Tony Rees and the Cottagers
18 Chas and Dave
19 Hi Tension
20 Winifred Atwell

ANSWERS

QUIZ 13 **SUNGLASSES**

1 Paul Weller of Style Council
2 Rocky Sharpe and the Replays
3 Andy Summers of Police
4 Nick Lowe
5 Korgis
6 Elton John
7 Dan Hartman

8 Les Gray
9 Ian Dury
10 Ray Charles
11 J. J. Cale
12 Rocky Burnette
13 Debbie Harry from Blondie
14 Neil Arthur

QUIZ 14 **THREE STEPS TO HEAVEN**

1 Madonna
2 Donovan
3 Dusty Springfield
4 Frank Sinatra
5 Rod Stewart
6 Culture Club
7 Beatles
8 Rolling Stones
9 Rockwell
10 Supremes
11 Prince
12 Debarge
13 Dionne Warwick
14 Fats Domino
15 Four Tops

16 Temptations
17 Kajagoogoo
18 Bob Dylan
19 Elvis Presley
20 Phil Collins
21 Dire Straits
22 Stevie Wonder
23 Lionel Richie
24 Don Henley
25 Nat "King" Cole
26 Queen
27 Spandau Ballet
28 Dean Martin
29 Fifth Dimension
30 Skeeter Davis

QUIZ 15 **HALFWAY TO PARADISE**

1 She's A Winner – Intruders
2 Shake Your Body – Jacksons
3 Love Action – Human League
4 The Lunatics – Funboy Three
5 Hello, This Is Joanie – Paul Evans
6 Love Grows – Edison Lighthouse
7 Dancing In The Moonlight – Thin Lizzy
8 Ain't Gonna Bump No More – Joe Tex
9 Can't Give You Anything – Stylistics
10 Tonight I'm Yours – Rod Stewart
11 Love Theme from 'A Star is Born' – Barbra Streisand
12 Old School Yard – Cat Stevens
13 Hands Up – Ottowan
14 Copacabana – Barry Manilow
15 It May Be Winter Outside – Love Unlimited
16 Rock 'n Roll – Kevin Johnson
17 Young Guns – Wham
18 Against All Odds – Phil Collins
19 Wherever I Lay My Hat – Paul Young
20 All Night Long – Lionel Richie

1. Theme from *Dr Kildare* – Richard Chamberlain
2. The Sideboard Song – Chas and Dave
3. I Love To Love – Tina Charles
4. Arthur's Theme – Christopher Cross
5. Sh-Boom – Darts and Crew-cuts (an extra mark for Chords)
6. Summer – Bobby Goldsboro
7. Give Me Love – George Harrison
8. I'm Just A Singer – Moody Blues
9. Shake Your Booty – KC and The Sunshine Band
10. Cacharpaya – Incantation
11. Captain Kremmen – Kenny Everett and Mike Vickers
12. Me And My Girl – David Essex
13. Number One – Tremeloes
14. Be Loud Be Proud – Toyah
15. Treason Teardrop – Explodes
16. Love is in Control – Donna Summer
17. Bridget The Midget – Ray Stevens
18. Mike Oldfield Single – Mike Oldfield
19. Wishing – A Flock Of Seagulls
20. Never Say Die – Cliff Richard

1. English Civil War – Clash
2. The Zoo – Commodores
3. Anyone For Tennis – Cream
4. Where Is The Love – Delegation
5. Mirror Mirror – Dollar
6. The River – Ken Dodd
7. Mr Raffles – Steve Harley and Cockney Rebel
8. Bad Case Of Lovin' You – Robert Palmer
9. Dick-A-Dum-Dum – Des O'Connor
10. L.O.D. – Billy Ocean
11. Can't Live With You – Mindbenders
12. I'll Give You The Earth – Keith Michell
13. Six Million Steps – Rahni Harris and F.L.O.
14. Ire Feelings – Rupie Edwards
15. Ossie's Dream – Tottenham Hotspur FA Cup Final Squad
16. Et Les Oiseaux Chantaient – Sweet People
17. Nuclear Device – Stranglers
18. Maid Of Orleans – Orchestral Manoeuvres in the Dark
19. Black Superman – Johnny Wakelin
20. Let There Be Peace On Earth – Michael Ward

QUIZ 16 **BAD OLD DAYS**

1. Toil
2. Week
3. Valley
4. Small
5. Cincinatti
6. Rocker
7. Drums
8. Tambourine
9. Lover's
10. Midas

ANSWERS

1	Flingel
2	Cow
3	Midnight
4	Cindy's
5	Sea
6	Martha
7	Crawl
8	Inspiration
9	Unite
10	Long

1	Mary
2	Better
3	Lonely
4	Cousins
5	Years
6	Love
7	Rags
8	Godiva
9	Yours
10	Changed

QUIZ 17 SATURDAY NIGHT AT THE MOVIES

1	Elvis Presley
2	Cliff Richard and the Shadows
3	Beatles
4	Elvis Presley
5	Gerry and the Pacemakers
6	Cliff Richard and the Shadows
7	John Travolta and Olivia Newton-John
8	Roger Daltrey, Ann-Margret and Oliver Reed, plus many others like Elton John and Tina Turner
9	Slade
10	Tommy Steele

11	Connie Francis
12	Elvis Presley
13	Beatles
14	Bee Gees
15	Little Richard
16	James Darren (or let yourself have a point for Duane Eddy as well)
17	Beatles
18	Jerry Lee Lewis
19	Irene Cara
20	Isaac Hayes

1	Gary Busey
2	George Hamilton
3	James Stewart
4	Tommy Steele
5	Diana Ross (the Lady being Billie Holiday, of course)
6	Roy Orbison
7	Shadows
8	Billy Fury
9	Tommy Steele
10	Dave Clark Five

11	*Beverley Hills Cop*
12	*The Woman In Red*
13	*Saturday Night Fever*
14	*Sgt Pepper's Lonely Hearts Club Band*
15	*Woodstock*
16	*It's Trad, Dad*
17	*The Girl Can't Help It*
18	*Viva Las Vegas*
19	*Twist Around The Clock*
20	*Stardust*

1   Mike Sarne
2   'Let's Hear It For The Boy' by Deniece Williams
3   *The Family Way* starring Hayley Mills and Hywel Bennett
4   *Change Of Habit*
5   *Rock Around The Clock, Don't Knock The Rock, American Hot Wax, Rock Rock Rock, Go Johnny Go* and *Mister Rock'n'Roll*
6   *Come September*
7   None were included in the films that inspired them
8   Yvonne Elliman
9   *The Blackboard Jungle*
10 *Disc Jockey Jamboree*
11 *The Blues Brothers*
12 *Expresso Bongo*
13 Sal Mineo
14 *Easy Rider*
15 *Watership Down* ('Bright Eyes' was the song). *Yellow Submarine* did not give rise to a number one hit, as the hit gave rise to the film
16 John Lennon
17 'Everybody's Talkin' by Nilsson
18 Elvis Presley, in *King Creole*
19 *To Sir With Love* (title song a number one for Lulu)
20 *The Rose* starring Bette Midler

QUIZ 18   DESPERATE BUT NOT SERIOUS

1   Mike Sarne (with Wendy Richard)
2   Dick Emery
3   Renee and Renato
4   Mike Reid (the other one)
5   Little Jimmy Osmond
6   Alexei Sayle
7   Steve Wright
8   Esther and Abi Ofarim
9   Lieutenant Pigeon
10 J. J. Barrie
11 Toy Dolls (Mandy Miller, who had the original success, never had a chart record of this classic, but her name is also acceptable as a correct answer)
12 Black Lace
13 Muppets featuring Kermit's cousin Robin
14 Shirley Ellis OR the Belle Stars (either correct)
15 Cockerel Chorus
16 Captain Sensible
17 Kenny Everett
18 Quantum Jump
19 Dennis Waterman and George Cole
20 Wombles

ANSWERS

1 Yin and Yan
2 David Gates
3 Wombles
4 Brighouse and Rastrick Brass Band, 'The Floral Dance'
5 Sue Wilkinson
6 B. A. Robertson
7 Tiny Tim
8 Jonathan King
9 'Hi De Hi (Holiday Rock)'
10 Peter Sellers
11 Sophia Loren
12 Chas and Dave
13 Smiley Culture
14 Goodies
15 Napoleon XIV
16 Keith Michell
17 Carl Malcolm
18 neil
19 Paul Burnett and Dave Lee Travis
20 Weird Al Yankovic sent up Michael Jackson

1 Ernie K-Doe
2 Kaye Sisters
3 Billie Davis
4 Krankies
5 Lance Percival
6 Bobby Bare
7 Larry Verne
8 *The Army Game*
9 'Here Comes The Judge'
10 'Big Nine'
11 RAH Band
12 Sheb Wooley ('Purple People Eater') and David Seville ('Witch Doctor')
13 Will Powers
14 'Ragtime Cowboy Joe'
15 Four Preps
16 Big Bad John
17 Hot Shots
18 Royal Teens
19 Ray Stevens
20 Chris Hill

QUIZ 19 THE LETTER

1 Ring Starr (Ringo Starr)
2 Bran Ferry (Bryan Ferry)
3 Nick Begs (Nick Beggs)
4 Ham! (Wham!)
5 Eton John (Elton John)
6 Pal McCartney (Paul McCartney)
7 Alison Moet (Alison Moyet)
8 Sad (Sade)
9 Mikey Crag (Mikey Craig)
10 Ton Hadley (Tony Hadley)
11 Bill Idol (Billy Idol)
12 Thompson Tins (Thompson Twins)
13 The Cash (The Clash)
14 Culture Cub (Culture Club)
15 Gay Kemp (Gary Kemp)
16 I'm On LeBon (Simon LeBon)
17 Wigs (Wings)
18 Ill Wyman (Bill Wyman)
19 By George (Boy George)
20 Vice Clarke (Vince Clarke)

1 Bin Crosby (Bing Crosby)
2 Ton Basil (Toni Basil)
3 Elaine Page (Elaine Paige)
4 Her Alpert (Herb Alpert)
5 Roy Ha (Roy Hay)
6 Wilson Picket (Wilson Pickett)
7 Rank Sinatra (Frank Sinatra)
8 Petula Lark (Petula Clark)
9 Earth Wind and Fir (Earth Wind and Fire)
10 Ken Odd (Ken Dodd)

11 Dane Eddy (Duane Eddy)
12 Plastic No Band (Plastic Ono Band)
13 Sandie Saw (Sandie Shaw)
14 Fleetwood Ma (Fleetwood Mac)
15 Men Corner (Amen Corner)
16 Chairmen of the Bard (Chairmen of the Board)
17 Everly Bothers (Everly Brothers)
18 Billy Fry (Billy Fury)
19 Ax Bygraves (Max Bygraves)
20 Nil Diamond (Neil Diamond)

1 Bach Boys (Beach Boys)
2 Race Kelly (Grace Kelly)
3 Berry Gory (Berry Gordy)
4 The Bet (The Beat)
5 Jams and Bobby Purify (James and Bobby Purify)
6 Rub Murray (Ruby Murray)
7 Tony Blackbun (Tony Blackburn)
8 Nat "Kin" Cole (Nat "King" Cole)
9 Acker Ilk (Acker Bilk)
10 Bobby Darn (Bobby Darin)
11 After the Ire (After the Fire)
12 Dave Dee, Dozy, Beaky, Mick and Tic (Dave Dee, Dozy, Beaky, Mick and Tich)
13 Fur Tops (Four Tops)
14 Book Benton (Brook Benton)
15 Frankie Line (Frankie Laine)
16 Water Brennan (Walter Brennan)
17 Frank Field (Frank Ifield)
18 Isle Brothers (Isley Brothers)
19 Rick Jams (Rick James)
20 Om Jones (Tom Jones)

QUIZ 20 **COMMUNICATION BREAKDOWN**

1 'Listen To The Radio (Atmosphere)'
2 'Telegraph'
3 'Radio Radio'
4 'A Star On A TV Show'
5 'Telegram Sam'
6 'Communication'
7 'The Letter'
8 'Telephone Line'
9 'Video Killed The Radio Star'
10 'Last Night a DJ Saved My Life'
11 'The Last Film'
12 'Turn Your Radio On'
13 'Please Mr Postman'
14 'Communication'
15 'I'm Gonna Sit Right Down And Write Myself A Letter'
16 'Telephone Man'
17 'Messages'
18 'The Telephone Always Rings'
19 'Pilot Of The Airwaves'
20 'On My Radio'

ANSWERS

QUIZ 21 **YOU DON'T HAVE TO BE IN THE ARMY TO FIGHT IN THE WAR**

1 Pat Benatar
2 Bob Marley and the Wailers
3 Wham!
4 Billy Bragg
5 Tubeway Army
6 Pipes and Drums of the Royal Scots Dragoon Guards
7 'A Scottish Soldier'
8 Tom Robinson
9 Culture Club
10 General Saint
11 Meco
12 'The Last Farewell'
13 Telly Savalas and Lee Marvin
14 Paul McCartney
15 **ABBA**
16 19
17 'Theme From M*A*S*H*'
18 Frankie Goes To Hollywood
19 Sgt Pepper
20 Jam

1 Captain Sensible, with 'Happy Talk' from *South Pacific*
2 Lieutenant Pigeon, with 'Mouldy Old Dough'
3 Major Lance, 'Um Um Um Um Um Um'
4 Edwin Starr
5 The Royal Navy ('Sailor')
6 General Custer ('Mr. Custer')
7 Running Bear's and Little White Dove's
8 Shirelles
9 *G. I. Blues*
10 Frank Sinatra
11 Jona Lewie
12 Staff Sergeant Barry Sadler
13 Johnny Horton and Lonnie Donegan
14 Buffy St Marie
15 14–18
16 'Happy Xmas (War Is Over)' by John and Yoko, the Plastic Ono Band and the Harlem Community Choir
17 Ken Thorne
18 T. Rex
19 Elvis Costello
20 Orchestral Manoeuvres In The Dark, with 'Enola Gay'

1. The US Marines
2. US53310761
3. Anthony Newley
4. Terry Dene
5. They were all serving at the time on *USS Essex*, so they called themselves The Essex
6. 'Lay Down Your Arms' by Anne Shelton
7. Admiral Halsey ('Uncle Albert/Admiral Halsey', which was never released as a single in UK)
8. 'When Johnny Comes Marching Home'
9. 'White Cliffs Of Dover'
10. Jimmy Cliff
11. Union Gap
12. 'Don't Cry My Love' (a hit for Vera Lynn)
13. 'He Was Beautiful'. Give yourself half a mark for 'Cavatina'
14. 'The Dam Busters March'
15. Country Joe and the Fish
16. Commodores
17. 'The Signature Tune Of The Army Game'
18. *Merry Christmas, Mr. Lawrence*
19. John Leyton
20. 'War Child'

QUIZ 22 **REMEMBER (THE DAYS OF THE OLD SCHOOL YARD)**

1. 'There's No One Quite Like Grandma'
2. Alice Cooper
3. Jam
4. 'Mull Of Kintyre'
5. Bronski Beat
6. Johnny Nash
7. Ramblers
8. 'Starmaker'
9. Jackson Five
10. Helen Shapiro
11. Clifford T. Ward
12. Musical Youth
13. 'Another Brick In The Wall (Part 2)'
14. Motorhead
15. 'Brown Sugar'
16. Boomtown Rats
17. 'Rock Around The Clock'
18. Jeannie C. Riley
19. 'Don't Stand So Close To Me'
20. Paul Miles-Kingston

1. 'I Don't Like Mondays'
2. 'School Day'
3. Sam Cooke
4. "Don't know much about history"
5. ABC
6. David Bowie
7. Yardbirds
8. Jethro Tull
9. *To Sir With Love*
10. Frank Ifield (in a song 'She Taught Me How To Yodel' which was never an A-side for Frank, but featured heavily in his act during his hit years – it was the B side of 'Lovesick Blues')
11. Jonathan King
12. Zombies
13. Damned
14. Bobby Rydell and Chubby Checker
15. Russ Conway
16. Smiths
17. Herman's Hermits
18. Rick Wakeman
19. Paul Simon
20. Crosby, Stills, Nash and Young

ANSWERS

1 Doris Day
2 Johnny Mathis
3 Gary "U.S." Bonds
4 Everly Brothers
5 A 'Bird Dog'
6 'D In Love'
7 Buddy Holly
8 Bobby Helms
9 Chubby Checker
10 Bobby Rydell
11 Bobby Vee

12 'Matchstalk Men and Matchstalk Cats and Dogs' by Brian and Michael
13 Connie Francis
14 Brenda Lee – 'Sweet Nothin's'
15 Otis Redding (an LP title of his)
16 Frank Sinatra
17 Bobby Darin
18 'Where Have All The Flowers Gone'
19 *King Creole* (star: Elvis Presley)
20 Allisons

QUIZ 23 UPTOWN FESTIVAL

1 'Diana' (Diana Ross)
2 'It's a Miracle' (Miracles)
3 'Which Way You Goin' Billy (Billy Preston)
4 'Jimmy Jimmy' (Jimmy Ruffin)
5 'Jackson' (Jermaine Jackson)
6 'I'm Gonna Be Strong' (Barret Strong)
7 'Claudette' (Claudette Robinson)
8 'Michael' (Michael Jackson)
9 'Message To Martha' (Martha Reeves)
10 'Temptation' (Temptations)

11 'Tammy' (Tammi Terrell)
12 'Seasons In The Sun' (Four Seasons)
13 'Top of the Pops' (Four Tops)
14 'Billy Don't Be A Hero' (Billy Griffin)
15 'Gaye' (Marvin Gaye)
16 'You Don't Have To Be A Star (To Be In My Show)' (Edwin Starr)
17 'William It Was Really Nothing' (William "Smokey" Robinson)
18 'Mary Had A Little Lamb' (Mary Wilson)
19 'The Dean And I' (R. Dean Taylor)
20 'I Don't Believe In Miracles' (Miracles)

1 'Martha My Dear' (Martha Reeves)
2 'How Long' (Shorty Long)
3 'Marvin The Paranoid Android' (Marvin Gaye)
4 'Mary Of The Fourth Form' (Mary Wells)
5 'Houston' (Thelma Houston)
6 'My Brother Martin' (Martin Luther King, whose speeches were recorded by Motown)
7 'Miracles' (Miracles)
8 'Diane' (Diane Earl)
9 'Marie Marie' (Teena Marie)
10 'Temptation' (Temptations)

11 'I Wonder Why' (Stevie Wonder)
12 'Sweet Seasons' (Four Seasons)
13 'James (Hold the Ladder Steady)' (Rick James)
14 'Bristol Stomp' (Johnny Bristol)
15 'What Will My Mary Say' (Mary Wells)
16 'Cut Across Shorty' (Shorty Long)
17 'Ronnie' (Ronnie White)
18 *Holland* (Brian Holland, Eddie Holland)
19 'Norman' (Norman Whitfield)
20 'Mrs. Robinson' (Claudette Robinson)

1 'Brenda' (Brenda Holloway)
2 'Please Don't Ask About Barbara' (Barbara Randolph)
3 'Viva Las Vegas' (Tata Vega)
4 'My Bonnie' (Bonnie Pointer)
5 'Bobby's Girl' (Bobby Taylor of Bobby Taylor and the Vancouvers)
6 'Dazz' (Dazz Band)
7 *Tommy* (Tommy Chong, later of Cheech and Chong)
8 'A Hundred Pounds Of Clay' (Tom Clay)
9 'Lovely Rita' (Rita Wright, later known as Syreeta)
10 'Temptation' (Temptations)

11 'Smoky Places' (William "Smokey Robinson)
12 'Eddie My Love' (Eddie Holland)
13 'Tall Paul' (Paul Williams of the Temptations)
14 'Little By Little' (Hattie Little)
15 'Washington Square' (Grover Washington Jr.)
16 'Give Me Some Truth' (Undisputed Truth)
17 'It Ain't The Meat It's The Motion' (Meat Loaf)
18 'I Wonder' (Stevie Wonder)
19 'John I'm Only Dancing' (Mabel John)
20 'Midnight Mary' (Mary Wells, whose hits included 'Two Lovers')

QUIZ 24 **A SOLID BOND IN YOUR HEART**

1 007
2 Matt Monro ('From Russia With Love')
3 M – 'Pop Muzik' and 'Moonlight and Muzak'
4 Ronnie Bond
5 Joyce Bond
6 Graham Bond
7 'Sock It To 'Em J.B.' – Rex Garvin and the Mighty Cravers
8 *On Her Majesty's Secret Service*
9 Herb Alpert
10 Tom Jones

QUIZ 25 **FAME**

1 Michael Caine
2 Aretha Franklin
3 Buddy Holly
4 Robert de Niro
5 Nelson Mandela
6 Muhammad Ali
7 Bo Diddley
8 'Nightshift' by the Commodores
9 'Missing You' by Diana Ross
10 Elvis Presley
11 Louis Quatorze
12 Stevie Wonder
13 Beethoven
14 Laurel and Hardy
15 Torvill and Dean
16 Sex Pistols
17 Duke Ellington
18 Hitler
19 Vincent van Gogh
20 The Red Baron (Baron von Richthofen)

1 Shakespeare
2 Buffalo Bill
3 Robin Hood
4 Alistair MacLeod ('Ally's Tartan Army')
5 Manchester United
6 Roy Orbison's wife Claudette
7 Einstein
8 West Ham United
9 King Midas
10 *Pat Garrett and Billy The Kid*
11 Smiley Lewis
12 Rasputin
13 Ma Baker
14 'Reasons To Be Cheerful, (Part 3)'
15 John F. Kennedy
16 Samson and Delilah
17 Eva Peron
18 Lady Godiva
19 Joan of Arc
20 Joltin' Joe

1 Laurence Olivier as Richard III
2 Stephen Biko
3 John Lennon, October 9
4 Sacha Distel
5 His son, Julian Lennon
6 Edgar Wallace
7 Aleister Crowley
8 Toulouse-Lautrec
9 Billie-Jean King, on 'Philadelphia Freedom'
10 'Melting Pot' by Blue Mink
11 Marvin (Gaye)
12 Max Yasgur
13 Don McLean
14 Queen Isabella of Spain
15 'Let's Think About Living' by Bob Luman
16 St Augustine
17 'John and Michie' – John and Michella Phillips of the Mamas and Papas
18 Dr Seuss
19 'Merry Xmas Everybody'
20 Bob Dylan

ANSWERS

QUIZ 26   **A PICTURE OF YOU**

1   Davy Jones of the Monkees
2   'Nobody Told Me'
3   Trevor Stanford
4   'Only The Lonely'/'It's Over'/'Oh Pretty Woman'
5   Billy J. Kramer and the Dakotas (Mike Mansfield)
6   Billy Fury
7   Rachel Sweet
8   'Great Balls Of Fire'
9   Swindon – they are XTC
10   Iggy Pop
11   David Cook
12   'Eve Of Destruction' by Barry McGuire
13   Swedish
14   Eric Stewart went on to join 10 C.C. who had their first five hits on Jonathan King's label UK. In 1985 he produced an album for Agnetha Faltskog from ABBA
15   Declan McManus
16   Chuck Berry
17   Left to right: Jean Jacques Burnel, Hugh Cornwell, Jet Black and Dave Greenfield
18   Racey
19   Captain Sensible (with Damned)
20   Freak (Number 23 in 1983)
21   Mick Talbot (now in Style Council)
22   'Three Steps to Heaven'
23   France
24   McFarlane
25   'You Turn Me On' (Ian Whitcomb)
26   Abbey Road
27   Buster Bloodvessel of Bad Manners
28   'One Day I'll Fly Away' (Number two in 1980). She is Randy Crawford
29   Steve Lawrence and Eydie Gorme
30   Les Compagnons De La Chanson
31   Leif Garrett
32   'Classical Gas' – Mason Williams
33   Gene Pitney
34   'Hungry Heart'
35   'Take Five', 'It's A Raggy Waltz'. Unsquare Dance'

QUIZ 27   **WE ARE THE WORLD**

1   Midge Ure
2   Bryan Ferry
3   Bob Dylan
4   John Lennon
5   To Me
6   Specials
7   'Mary's Boy Child'
8   Sarah Brightman and Paul Miles-Kingston
9   USA For Africa
10   Michael Jackson and Lionel Richie
11   Culture Club
12   Paul McCartney and Stevie Wonder
13   Blue Mink
14   'The Times They Are A-Changin''
15   Barry McGuire
16   His Lord
17   'Give Peace A Chance'
18   Edwin Hawkins Singers
19   Tom Robinson
20   Grandmaster Flash and Melle Mel

1 ABBA	11 Al Green
2 Bob Dylan	12 Hedgehoppers Anonymous
3 Manfred Mann	13 Jonathan King
4 Martin Luther King	14 Elvis Presley
5 Wings	15 Gay rights
6 'The Night They Drove Old Dixie Down'	16 Kinks
7 'There But For Fortune'	17 The 'Love Train'
8 Strawbs	18 Ray Stevens
9 Bob Dylan	19 Stevie Wonder
10 Specials	20 Peter Sarstedt

1 Bob and Marcia	8 The Who
2 "Bent and paralysed" – an Asian war victim	9 In The Heart Of The City
3 He was mugged	10 Donovan
4 Joystrings	11 Norman "Hurricane" Smith
5 Chi-Lites	12 Crosby, Stills, Nash and Young
6 Orioles (a R & B hit in the US in 1953) but if you said Artie Glenn who wrote 'Crying In The Chapel' or either Darrell Glenn or Rex Allen who each had country hits with the song in 1953, you should be compiling these questions, not answering them. Elvis Presley is the wrong answer	13 Wink Martindale
	14 James Brown
	15 Wille Nelson
	16 Simon and Garfunkel
	17 Edwin Starr
	18 Frijid Pink
	19 David Bowie ('Heroes')
7 The Universal Soldier	20 Pete Seeger

QUIZ 28 **BE STIFF**

1 'You'll Always Find Me In The Kitchen at Parties'
2 'Hit Me With Your Rhythm Stick'
3 'Watching The Detectives'
4 Kirsty MacColl
5 Rachel Sweet
6 Ian Dury
7 'House Of Fun'
8 'They Don't Know'
9 Barbara Gaskin
10 'Pretend'
11 Ten Pole Tudor
12 *New Boots and Panties!!*
13 Madness, 'My Girl'
14 'Stop The Cavalry'
15 'Reasons To Be Cheerful'
16 *My Aim Is True*
17 Damned
18 'Lucky Number'
19 'Alison'
20 Pat Boone

ANSWERS

1 Nick Lowe
2 Adverts
3 Colin Blunstone
4 *Work Rest and Play*
5 Ian Gomm
6 'Less Than Zero'
7 'What A Waste'
8 Alberto y Lost Trios Paranoias
9 Wreckless Eric
10 Terry Dactyl and the Dinosaurs ('Seaside Shuffle')
11 'Leavin' Here'
12 Clare, Jennie, Judy, Sarah-Jane, Miranda, Lesley, or Stella
13 'One Step Beyond'
14 'New Toy'
15 'Jocko Homo'
16 1982
17 Lene Lovich
18 *Oklahoma!*
19 *The Wit and Wisdom of Ronald Reagan*
20 Stiff Little Fingers

1 Nick Lowe
2 'It's You, Only You' by Lene Lovich
3 Any Trouble
4 Joe 'King' Carrasco
5 Davey Payne
6 'Throwing My Baby Out With The Bathwater'
7 Lew Lewis
8 Larry Wallis
9 Tyla Gang
10 Booji Boy
11 Lene Lovich, Mickey Jupp, Wreckless Eric, Jona Lewie, Rachel Sweet
12 It was actually a photo of Eddie and the Hot Rods
13 Richard Hell
14 Wreckless Eric
15 Dave Edmunds
16 Mick Farren
17 Mickey Jupp
18 Pink Fairies
19 Rumour
20 Huey Lewis and the News

QUIZ 29 BACK TO THE SIXTIES

1 Wayne Fontana and the Mindbenders
2 Peter and Gordon
3 Rolling Stones
4 Beatles
5 Yardbirds
6 The Who
7 Andy Williams
8 Them
9 Georgie Fame
10 Unit Four Plus Two
11 Kinks
12 Sonny and Cher
13 Ken Dodd
14 Walker Brothers
15 Hollies
16 Elvis Presley
17 Everly Brothers
18 Byrds
19 Roger Miller
20 Cliff Richard

ANSWERS

1. Manfred Mann
2. Peter and Gordon
3. Cliff Richard
4. Cliff Richard
5. Elvis Presley
6. Supremes
7. Pretty Things
8. Dave Clark Five (interestingly, the first of two hits he had with different songs of this title; the second was in 1967)
9. Tom Jones
10. Searchers
11. Searchers
12. Searchers
13. Shadows
14. Dave Dee, Dozy, Beaky, Mick and Tich
15. Four Tops
16. Herman's Hermits
17. Honeycombs
18. Ivy League
19. Kinks
20. Temptations

1. Searchers
2. Nashville Teens
3. *Help!* (The Beatles)
4. *The Beatles At The Hollywood Bowl*
5. They were all recorded by artists with surnames beginning "Mc" – Barry McGuire, the McCoys, Paul McCartney
6. Gary Lewis and the Playboys
7. Sonny and Cher – they recorded 'Baby Don't Go' as Caesar and Cleo before they hit with 'I Got You Babe'. 'Baby Don't Go' was then re-issued under their hit names, becoming a number 11 hit in the UK. But the names of Caesar and Cleo never graced the charts
8. Nat "King" Cole and Stubby Kaye
9. Tom Jones – *Thunderball*
10. Spokesmen
11. Chubby Checker and Freddie and The Dreamers
12. Houston
13. Bob Dylan, Rolling Stones and Beatles
14. Twinkle
15. P. F. Sloan
16. Silkie
17. A toughie – 'Poupee De Cire, Poupee De Son' by France Gall, representing Luxembourg
18. 'I Belong' – Kathy Kirby
19. Joan Baez
20. Birds – an English act, attempted to sue the American Byrds for using their name – a publicity stunt that did not achieve a great deal for the British group

QUIZ 30 **JOIN TOGETHER**

The blanks should be filled in by:

'I Don't Know Why'; 'My Cherie Amour'; 'I Just Called To Say I Love You'; 'Three Coins In The Fountain'; 'My Way'; 'Diana'; 'It Doesn't Matter Anymore'; 'That'll Be The Day'; 'Love's Made A Fool Of You'; 'La Bamba'; 'Donna'; 'Come On Let's Go'; 'Singing The Blues'; 'Cherry Pink and Apple Blossom White'; 'This Ole House'; 'Green Door'; 'Blue Christmas'; 'I Can Help'; 'Don't Be Cruel'; 'Love Me Tender'

A N S W E R S

The connections we are looking for are:

1 They duet on the number one hit 'Easy Lover'
2 They both hit with 'You Can't Hurry Love'
3 They both hit with different songs called 'You Keep Me Hanging On'
4 They duetted on 'Suddenly'
5 They both sang for Britain in Eurovision Song Contest
6 They both recorded 'A Man Without Love'
7 They both had hits with titles in French: Engelbert with 'Les Bicyclettes De Belsize' and Siouxsie with 'Il Est Ne Le Divin Enfant'
8 The Creatures are Siouxsie Sioux and Budgie
9 Both are duos who hit with "Mad" songs – 'Mad Eyed Screamer' and 'Mad World'
10 Half of Tears For Fears is Curt Smith
11 Both hit with versions of 'Mack The Knife'
12 Darin wrote 'Early In The Morning' by Holly
13 Holly hit with 'Bo Diddley'
14 Pretty Things took their name from a Bo Diddley song
15 Both hit with "Midnight" songs – 'Midnight To Six Man' and 'Midnight Train To Georgia'
16 Both recorded for Motown
17 Wonder's 'Masterblaster (Jammin')' was a tribute to Marley, using the Marley song
18 Clapton hit number one in the States with Marley's 'I Shot The Sheriff'
19 They were both in Cream
20 Bruce was a part of Manfred Mann for a time
21 d'Abo was lead singer after Paul Jones left
22 They both sang on the original *Jesus Christ Superstar* album
23 So did Murray Head
24 Ulvaeus co-wrote Head's 'One Night In Bangkok'
25 Ulvaeus was a quarter of ABBA
26 Blancmange hit with ABBA's 'The Day Before You Came'
27 The Searchers hit with 'Sweets For My Sweet', which is an awful pun with Blancmange
28 Both acts had three number ones and one number two with four consecutive releases (and they both came from Liverpool)
29 Only Gerry and Frankie have had three number ones and a number two with their first four releases
30 Both hit number one with a Rodgers and Hammerstein song
31 Sensible played in the Damned
32 The Damned hit with 'Love Song' and PIL with 'This Is Not A Love Song'
33 Both include Johnny Rotten
34 Both managed by Malcolm MacLaren
35 Boy George sang with both acts
36 Boy George and Jon Moss both performed on the Band Aid single
37 Bob Geldof is the only person who performed on both records, but the USA for Africa project was inspired by the success of Band Aid
38 Jackson co-wrote the song 'We Are The World'
39 They duetted on 'Say Say Say' and 'The Girl Is Mine'
40 McCartney was a Beatle
41 Earth Wind And Fire hit with the Beatles song, 'Got To Get You Into My Life'
42 Philip Bailey is Earth Wind and Fire's drummer

These are the connections we were thinking of, but you may come up with perfectly acceptable alternatives, in which case award yourself 2 points anyway

QUIZ 31 NOTHING RHYMED

1	Shadows	11	Acker Bilk
2	Duane Eddy	12	Kenny Ball and his Jazzmen
3	String-a-longs	13	Jet Harris and Tony Meehan
4	Beatles (a track on the *Magical Mystery Tour* double EP)	14	Mr Bloe
5	Mike Oldfield	15	Russ Conway
6	Space	16	Percy Faith
7	Shadows	17	Isaac Hayes
8	Peppers	18	Violinski
9	Jean-Michel Jarre	19	Pipes and Drums and The Military Band of the Royal Scots Dragoon Guards
10	Manuel and his Music of the Mountains	20	Blackbyrds

1	Floyd Cramer	12	Herb Alpert
2	Duane Eddy	13	Average White Band
3	Focus	14	Nice
4	Joe Henderson	15	Booker T and the MGs
5	Floyd Cramer	16	Sounds Orchestral (but we'll also let you have Vince Guaraldi Trio, who hit in the US two years before Sounds Orchestral's 1965 worldwide smash)
6	Shadows		
7	Tornados		
8	Winifred Atwell		
9	Roger Williams	17	Nini Rosso
10	Peter Nero	18	Sandy Nelson
11	Russ Conway	19	Bill Doggett
		20	Duane Eddy

1 Barry White
2 Marketts
3 Fratton Park is where Portsmouth Football Club play. Mike Oldfield had a big instrumental hit with 'Portsmouth'
4 Perez Prado
5 Spyro Gyra
6 Duane Eddy
7 Bobby Darin
8 Chantays
9 'Pipeline'
10 Walter Murphy and the Big Apple Band
11 Kaiser Bill's Batman
12 Buddy Holly – the composer/producer was Norman Petty
13 *Variations*
14 Winifred Atwell
15 Shadows – five
16 Rick Wakeman
17 Acker Bilk ('Summer Set' was the title of his first hit)
18 Van McCoy
19 Joe Meek
20 Dakotas

ANSWERS

QUIZ 32 HERE IS THE NEWS

1 'New York City'
2 'News At Ten'
3 'News Of The World'
4 'New World Man'
5 'New Life'
6 'Brand New Key'
7 'You Make Me Feel Brand New'
8 'New Orleans'
9 'New York Mining Disaster 1941'
10 'New Kid In Town'
11 'A New Fashion'
12 'New York New York'
13 'New Amsterdam'
14 'It's Good News Week'
15 'Keepin' Love New'
16 'Something Old Something New'
17 'New Song'
18 'New Moon On Monday'
19 'A New Day'
20 'New World In The Morning'

QUIZ 33 VIDEO KILLED THE RADIO STAR

1 Roland Rat
2 Billy Connolly
3 Hutch (David Soul)
4 *Top Of The Pops*
5 *Hill Street Blues*
6 *The Young Ones*
7 Alexei Sayle
8 'Arthur Daley ('E's Alright)'
9 'Theme From Harry's Game'
10 'Eye Level' by Simon Park
11 Monkees
12 'The Smurf Song' by Father Abraham and the Smurfs
13 Wombles
14 Kids From 'Fame'
15 'Grandad' by Clive Dunn
16 Muppets
17 *Magical Mystery Tour*
18 'That's Livin' Alright' by Joe Fagin
19 'Snot Rap'
20 Fraggles

1 'Postman Pat'
2 'What Are We Gonna Get 'Er Indoors'
3 'Whispering Grass' by Windsor Davies and Don Estelle
4 *Crossroads*
5 'In The Ghetto'
6 'Theme from M*A*S*H*'
7 'Get Away' by Georgie Fame
8 'I Can't Let Maggie Go' by Honeybus
9 'Chariots Of Fire' by Vangelis
10 Archies
11 Godiego
12 'Step Inside Love'
13 'Something Tells Me (Something's Gonna Happen Tonight)'
14 'I'd Like To Teach The World To Sing'
15 Shakin' Stevens
16 Goodies
17 Michael Buerk
18 Henry Mancini
19 Juan Martin
20 Partridge Family

1 *Compact*
2 Anthony Newley
3 'Johnny Remember Me' by John Leyton
4 Andrew Lloyd Webber
5 'Love Me Tender'
6 'Three Stars Will Shine Tonight'
7 Noel Edmonds
8 'Tomboy'
9 Wilfred Brambell and Harry H. Corbett (*Steptoe and Son*)
10 Julie Covington, Rula Lenska, Charlotte Cornwell and Sue Jones-Davies
11 Richard Denton and Martin Cook
12 Donovan
13 *The Army Game*
14 *The Six Wives of Henry VIII*
15 *Whatever Happened To The Likely Lads* NOT *The Likely Lads*
16 John Inman, 'Are You Being Served Sir'
17 Joe Loss
18 Johnny Keating and Norrie Paramor
19 'The Gambler' by Kenny Rogers
20 'Stranger On The Shore' by Acker Bilk

QUIZ 34   I CALL YOUR NAME

1 Wham	11 Kajagoogoo
2 Rolling Stones	12 Frankie Goes To Hollywood
3 Everly Brothers	13 Daryl Hall and John Oates
4 **ABBA**	14 Bronski Beat
5 Cream	15 Eurythmics
6 Carpenters	16 Pretenders
7 Culture Club	17 Thompson Twins
8 Queen	18 Supremes
9 Simon and Garfunkel	19 Duran Duran
10 10 C.C.	20 Fleetwood Mac

1 Spandau Ballet	11 Labelle
2 Led Zeppelin	12 Monkees
3 Crickets	13 Pink Floyd
4 Steely Dan	14 Peter, Paul and Mary
5 Genesis	15 Pointer Sisters
6 Bad Company	16 Mamas and Papas
7 Band	17 Lovin' Spoonful
8 Bonzo Dog Doo-Dah Band	18 Temptations
9 Who	19 Fame and Price Together
10 Brinsley Schwarz	20 Emerson, Lake and Palmer

1 Average White Band	11 Sadistic Mika Band
2 Creedence Clearwater Revival	12 Seals and Crofts
3 Crosby, Stills, Nash and Young	13 Carter Family
4 Isley Brothers	14 Mud
5 Kiss	15 Kingston Trio
6 Little Feat	16 ZZ Top
7 Manhattan Transfer	17 Staple Singers
8 Buggles	18 Fifth Dimension
9 Nazareth	19 Flatt and Scruggs
10 Young Rascals	20 Andrews Sisters

ANSWERS

QUIZ 35 **ALL THOSE YEARS AGO**

1	Still
2	Voodoo
3	Fighting
4	Daddy
5	Something
6	Float
7	Baker
8	Star
9	Miracle
10	Dudes

1	Jarrow
2	Angie
3	Hurt
4	Greased
5	America
6	Adolescence
7	Suburbs
8	Grandma's
9	Box
10	Honestly

1	Dios
2	Dippety
3	Mexican
4	World
5	Low
6	Reggae
7	10538
8	Jane
9	Spanner
10	Know

QUIZ 36 **JACK AND DIANE**

(Ring, Ring)

DIANE: Hello

VOICE: Hello, how are you? *My name is Jack. Oh Diane, I just called to say I love you.

DIANE: Hey! Baby, how sweet it is *to love somebody *endlessly as I love you.

HAPPY JACK: Oh you pretty thing! You don't have to say you love me. I know we are in love.

DIANE: You took the words right out of my mouth, my friend Jack. What am I gonna do with you Saturday nite?

HAPPY JACK: We can work it out the next time I feel love comin' on. If I said you had a beautiful body, would you hold it against me, you sexy thing.

DIANE: *Oh no. You're so vain. I'm gonna run away from you if you believe I'm you're puppet. I'm not your stepping stone. *Love is a many-splendoured thing. What you're proposing *ain't nothing like the real thing, randy Scouse git.

JUMPING JACK FLASH: What'd I say, woman? I'm not a juvenile delinquent. I'm a man *and I love you so. Will you love me tomorrow?

DIANE: Will I what?

JACKIE: Let's get together again tomorrow night. How does that grab you, darlin'?

ANSWERS

DIANE: You drive me crazy, Girls just wanna have fun, that's all. You can't hurry love if you wanna be happy. I'll get by without you.

JUMPING JACK FLASH: But you're mine....

DIANE: *Fing's ain't what they used to be. Hit the road, Jack. Goodbye-ee.

JILTED JOHN: Don't hang up. Baby please don't go. Don't.

(The sound of silence)

SMOOTH OPERATOR: She's gone.

The asterisked clues give the first letters: M T E O L A A F, which rearranged spell the name of the man who recorded 'You Took The Words Right Out Of My Mouth', Meat Loaf.

QUIZ 37 THREE STARS

1	Mary	11	Jam
2	Roll	12	Police
3	Boo	13	Len Barry
4	Palmer	14	Trio
5	Fire	15	Da Da Da
6	Walker Brothers	16	Frankie Goes To Hollywood
7	Crosby, Stills and Nash	17	Commodores
8	Cream	18	Thompson Twins
9	Bananarama	19	Pointer Sisters
10	Bee Gees	20	Supremes

1	'Vici'	10	Wings
2	Billy	11	Ronettes
3	Reynolds	12	Ronettes
4	James Ingram	13	Wings
5	Temptations (not Four Tops – that combo was Supremes and Four Tops – no Diana)	14	Goodies
		15	Beverley Sisters
		16	Ivy League
6	Chuck Berry	17	Imagination
7	Beach Boys	18	Stray Cats
8	ABBA	19	'Three Steps To Heaven'
9	ABBA	20	Björn Ulvaeus, Tim Rice and Benny Andersson

1	Poni-Tails	12	Frank Ifield (who was born in England, not Australia)
2	Bachelors	13	Three Degrees
3	Tennessee Two	14	ZZ Top
4	Velvelettes	15	Sister Rose
5	Ivy Three	16	Big Three
6	Kingston Trio	17	Creedence Clearwater Revival
7	Three Dog Night	18	Browns
8	Rush	19	Scaffold (in their hit 'Thank You Very Much')
9	Giorgio Moroder		
10	Jets	20	Rod, Dave (with Barbara Gaskin – not the Dave of the Eurythmics) and Amii
11	Olivia Newton-John		

A N S W E R S

QUIZ 38 (CALL ME) NUMBER ONE

1 'Jump'
2 'Hello'
3 'Footloose'
4 *Purple Rain*
5 Huey Lewis
6 'Karma Chameleon'
7 Ray Parker Jr.
8 *Thriller*

9 'Wake Me Up Before You Go Go'
10 'I Just Called To Say I Love You'
11 Lionel Richie and Michael Jackson
12 Phil Collins
13 Julio Iglesias
14 'Like A Virgin'
15 George Michael and Andrew Ridgeley
16 'Dancing In The Dark'

1 Nickolas and Valerie
2 'Smalltown Boy'
3 'Waiting For A Girl Like You'
4 Lionel Richie
5 'Say Say Say', a duet with Michael Jackson
6 'Time After Time'
7 Billy Ocean
8 'Keep On Loving You'

9 Frankie Beverly
10 Rick James
11 'When Doves Cry'
12 Capitol
13 Babys
14 Marvin Gaye and Jackie Wilson
15 *Requiem*
16 *Sports*

1 Wham Featuring George Michael
2 'Owner Of A Lonely Heart' by Yes
3 1960
4 'Let's Go Crazy'
5 Don Myrick
6 'Too Much Too Little Too Late', a duet with Johnny Mathis
7 'Out Of Touch'
8 Jenny Burton

9 Willie Nelson
10 They were on the two sides of the first number one on the 12″ chart
11 Escovedo
12 Kevin Cronin
13 'This Is My Night'
14 Steve Goodman
15 *No Jacket Required*
16 Santana

QUIZ 39 STAR ON A TV SHOW

1 *Top Of The Pops*
2 *Ready Steady Go*
3 *Thank Your Lucky Stars*
4 *The Tube*
5 *Revolver*
6 *Pop Quiz*
7 *Old Grey Whistle Test*
8 *Boy Meets Girl*
9 *Six-Five Special*
10 *Oxford Road Show*

1. *Ready Steady Win*
2. *Pop Quest*
3. John Barry wrote the *Juke Box Jury* theme ('Hit and Miss') and David Jacobs presented the show
4. Barry Fantoni
5. Alistair hosts the TV show *Razzamatazz* and Quincy had a hit with a record of the same name
6. *All Systems Freeman*
7. Sally James
8. *Discwizz*
9. Jimmy Savile
10. Tony Palmer

1. Tony Blackburn
2. Cephas Howard of Temperance Seven
3. *Man In The Moon*
4. Scotland
5. 'Love And Fury' by the Tornados
6. *Old Grey Whistle Test*
7. *Drumbeat*
8. *Six-Five Special*
9. *Oh Boy*
10. *Thank Your Lucky Stars*

QUIZ 40 **STRANGE BREW**

1. Roland Orzabal: not Culture Club
2. David Ball: not Wham!
3. Paul Young: has had a solo number one by May 1985
4. 'She Loves You': the only number one hit
5. 'The Reflex': the only number one hit
6. Alison Moyet: not American
7. Brian May: not a drummer
8. *No Jacket Required*: by Phil Collins, not Paul Young
9. Queen For Tonight: not from *Chess*
10. Little Richard: not Big
11. Lionel Richie: has not duetted with Paul McCartney
12. Eurythmics: never produced by Trevor Horn
13. Yellow Dog: the others are snakes
14. 'Penny Lane': not also an album title
15. 'Girls On Film': not from *Rio* album
16. Thelma Houston: not a Marvin Gaye duettist
17. 'I'm The One': not a number one
18. Wanda: not a member of the Jackson family
19. 'School's Out': not banned by the BBC
20. 'The Jean Genie': not a number one

ANSWERS

1 Satisfaction: written by Mick Jagger and Keith Richard
2 Jonathan King: the other two are the same man
3 RCA: not an EMI label (although was once distributed through HMV)
4 'All My Loving': not on *Please Please Me* LP
5 Billy Preston: never drummed with the Beatles
6 Fox: did not hit with 'Only You'
7 Spencer Davis Group: never featured Eric Clapton
8 Maurice Gibb: never had a solo hit. Barry Gibb as the non-twin worth half marks
9 'Nice One Cyril': not performed by a football team
10 Elvis Presley: the only one to use his real name
11 Searchers: not produced by George Martin
12 *Welcome To The Pleasuredome*: proceeds not given to charity
13 Piglets: Jonathan King does not perform on their hit
14 'I See The Moon': not number one in two versions
15 Nino Tempo and April Stevens: brother and sister, not husband and wife
16 Go West: their name is not the same word twice
17 Billy Fury: does not have a brother who had a solo hit
18 Nicole: not a one-hit wonder
19 John McNally: plays rhythm guitar, not bass
20 'Hello Goodbye': not part of a double-sided number one

1 Bob Dylan: no hit single called 'Tonight'
2 Steve Miller: no hit with an unnamed female vocalist
3 Elvis Presley: never issued a single written by Jagger and Richard
4 'City Of New Orleans': a train not a ship
5 Freddie Garrity: never hit number one
6 Byrds: never had a Jones in the group
7 Andy Williams: his surname has more than seven letters
8 Marty Wilde: not born on February 17
9 Tommy Zang: American, and a vocalist not an instrumentalist
10 Michael Jackson: Jackson is not a capital city
11 Finland: has never won the Eurovision Song Contest
12 Detroit Wheels: New York and Buffalo are in New York State, Detroit isn't
13 Manfred Mann: never a member of John Mayall's Bluesbreakers
14 Downliners Sect: did not feature Mick Fleetwood on drums
15 Johnny Preston: no Red Indian blood
16 Real Thing: all the others have had hit singles on at least four labels
17 *A Trick Of The Trail*: not a number one LP
18 'Goodbye': not a David Essex hit
19 Hollies: never hit with a Lennon/McCartney song (although they did with a George Harrison number)
20 Three Degrees: not a part of the Philadelphia All-Stars hit: 'Let's Clean Up The Ghetto'

These are the answers we were looking for, although you may find alternative answers that would be acceptable

QUIZ 41 **PRIZE OF GOLD**

1 'You Light Up My Life'	11 San Francisco
2 'Mack The Knife'	12 'This Will Be'
3 'Sailing'	13 1967
4 Cyndi Lauper	14 Culture Club
5 Tammy Wynette	15 George Benson
6 'Afternoon Delight'	16 *Car Wash*
7 Carole King	17 Sir Georg Solti
8 Jimmy Savile	18 'Killing Me Softly With His Song'
9 'Better Be Good To Me'	19 *A Summer Place*
10 *Let It Be*	20 Peggy Lee

1 Terry Britten and Graham Lyle
2 'Volare'
3 Henry Mancini
4 Carnegie Hall
5 George Harrison, Ravi Shankar, Bob Dylan, Leon Russell, Ringo Starr, Billy Preston, Eric Clapton and Klaus Voormann
6 *Songs in the Key of Life*
7 'Soul Man'
8 'Dominique'
9 Lou Adler
10 David Cassidy
11 'Live And Let Die'
12 Kenny Loggins and Michael McDonald
13 'Without You'
14 Thom Bell
15 Stan Getz
16 Fifth Dimension
17 'I Want To Hold Your Hand'
18 Stephen Sondheim
19 Bob Newhart
20 'People'

1 Best Recording for Children	11 Geoff Emerick
2 Jimmy Driftwood	12 Pete Hamill
3 Jimmy Bowen	13 Piano
4 'A Taste of Honey'	14 Winstons
5 Ferrante and Teicher	15 'Love Of The Common People'
6 Andrew Gold	16 'Heaven's Just A Sin Away'
7 'Alley Cat'	17 *Rumours* by Fleetwood Mac
8 'The Entertainer'	18 'I Can't Stop Loving You'
9 'The Way We Were'	19 Eumir
10 Pointer Sisters	20 Billy May

ANSWERS

QUIZ 42 **ONE OF US**

Elvis Presley, Lulu and The Luvvers, Linda Lewis, Paul McCartney, Peter and Gordon, Paul Gambaccini, Dave Dee, Scritti Politti, Julian Lennon, Julian Lloyd Webber, Björn and Benny (ABBA), Rock 'n Roll, Hank and Bruce (Shadows), Dave Clark, Paul Hardcastle – this leaves "Pete" as the odd one out

Johnny Rotten, Sid Vicious, Duran Duran, Me and Bobby McGee, Boy George, Ron Wood, Roy Wood, Hissing Sid, Renee and Renato, Paul Simon, Simon Le Bon, Andy Williams, Chad and Jeremy, Joe Jackson, George Michael – this leaves "Terry" as the odd one out

Ten Pole Tudor, Ten Years After, Love and Pride, Benny and The Jets, Ace Kefford, Elaine (Paige) and Barbara (Dickson), Paul King, Terry Jacks, Barbra (Streisand) and Neil (Diamond), Barbra (Streisand) and Donna (Summer), Jonathan King, Randy Jackson, Jackson Five, Bohemian Rhapsody, Ten C.C. – this leaves "Queen" as the odd one out

QUIZ 43 **CALLING YOUR NAME**

1	Diana	11	David Watts
2	Billie Jean	12	Angelo
3	Jane	13	Figaro
4	Fernando	14	Eileen
5	Juliet	15	Billy
6	Lily	16	Layla
7	Lucille	17	Prudence
8	Lucille	18	Father Christmas
9	Dolly	19	Tom
10	Pat	20	Johnny B. Goode

1 Rosanna
2 Robin
3 Louise
4 Joanna
5 Rikki
6 John
7 William
8 Alfie
9 Bennie
10 Candida
11 Mary
12 Daniel
13 Denis
14 Emma
15 John
16 Lola
17 Michelle
18 Mickey
19 Carol
20 Diane

1 Jessie
2 Spotty Muldoon
3 Lucy Jordan
4 Paladin
5 Bertha
6 Cindy
7 Enola Gay
8 Georgy Girl
9 Jimmy
10 Mary Ellen
11 Vic
12 Jolene
13 Lana
14 James
15 Patricia
16 Joe
17 Nelson
18 Simon Smith
19 Guitar George
20 Jimmy Brown

QUIZ 44 A LITTLE BIT MORE

1 Madam Ant (Adam Ant)
2 March Almond (Marc Almond)
3 Band Paid (Band Aid)
4 Salt Solo (Sal Solo)
5 Shade (Sade)
6 Sandie Shawl (Sandie Shaw)
7 Stalk Talk (Talk Talk)
8 Prod Stewart (Rod Stewart)
9 Brush (Rush)
10 Frockwell (Rockwell)

11 Chris Real (Chris Rea)
12 Belt-on John (Elton John)
13 Boomtown Rants (Boomtown Rats)
14 New Border (New Order)
15 Bray Parker Jr (Ray Parker Jr)
16 Part Company (Art Company)
17 Prose Royce (Rose Royce)
18 Diana Cross (Diana Ross)
19 Donna Slummer (Donna Summer)
20 Tracey Pullman (Tracey Ullman)

1 Kiki Deep (Kiki Dee)
2 Shot Chocolate (Hot Chocolate)
3 Lou Greed (Lou Reed)
4 Cleo Sayer (Leo Sayer)
5 Swings (Wings)
6 Warp (War)
7 Joe Trex (Joe Tex)
8 Trams (Tams)
9 Billy Swank (Billy Swan)
10 All Stewart (Al Stewart)

11 Steely Dane (Steely Dan)
12 Vain Morrison (Van Morrison)
13 Meant Loaf (Meat Loaf)
14 Tamil Lynn (Tami Lynn)
15 Greg Flake (Greg Lake)
16 Pal Green (Al Green)
17 Randy Gibb (Andy Gibb)
18 Part Garfunkel (Art Garfunkel)
19 Devon (Devo)
20 Boney Ma (Boney M)

ANSWERS

1 Four Stops (Four Tops)
2 Crick Nelson (Rick Nelson)
3 Sonny and Cheer (Sonny and Cher)
4 Frank Weird (Frank Weir)
5 Mary Swells (Mary Wells)
6 Genie Pitney (Gene Pitney)
7 Lesley Gored (Lesley Gore)
8 Pate Boone (Pat Boone)
9 Tommy Rope (Tommy Roe)
10 Same and Dave (Sam and Dave)

11 Alp Saxon (Al Saxon)
12 Tiny Time (Tiny Tim)
13 Theme (Them)
14 Vanity Flare (Vanity Fare)
15 Bobby Veer (Bobby Vee)
16 Zager and Evians (Zager and Evans)
17 Lent Barry (Len Barry)
18 Bleach Boys (Beach Boys)
19 Bee Geese (Bee Gees)
20 Stony Bennett (Tony Bennett)

QUIZ 45 **PARTY PARTY**

1 'Stand Down Margaret'
2 John F. Kennedy
3 'My Guy' by Tracey Ullman
4 Disraeli (*Disraeli Gears*)
5 'Anarchy In The UK'
6 'Michael' (Heseltine)
7 Napoleon XIV
8 'Party Fears Two'
9 'Elected'
10 'A Day In The Life'

11 'Abraham Martin And John'
12 'Maggie's Farm'
13 'This Ole House'
14 Big Brother and the Holding Company
15 'Party'
16 Members
17 'Power To The People'
18 'Ball Of Confusion'
19 'Between The Wars'
20 'House Of Fun'

1 'Garden Of Eden'
2 'Jesse' (Jackson)
3 Parliament
4 'House Of The Rising Sun'
5 'Nice One Cyril'
6 'Leaving On A Jet Plane'
7 'Passion'
8 'Ronnie'
9 'Harry Truman'
10 Gang of Four

11 'The Times They Are A-Changin''
12 Supremes (Mary Wilson was a member)
13 Shirley and Company
14 'If I Ruled The World'
15 *Talking Book*
16 'Movin' Out (Anthony's Song)'
17 Premiers
18 'Does Your Chewing Gun Lose Its Flavour?'
19 'House On Fire'
20 'Ol' MacDonald'

1 'Dancing In The Dark'
2 'Battle Of New Orleans'
3 *The First Family*
4 'Steel Men'
5 'Hot Rod Lincoln'
6 'Oh Lord, Why Lord'
7 'Open The Door Richard'
8 ''Minister of the New Super Heavy Funk''
9 'MTA'
10 *The Wit and Wisdom of Ronald Reagan*

11 The Presidents
12 'The Party's Over'
13 'The Madison'
14 Senator Bobby
15 'Party Pops'
16 'Sweet William'
17 'Jimmy Unknown'
18 'Washington Square'
19 Robert Kennedy
20 Donald Peers

QUIZ 46   IT'S NOW OR NEVER

1 Music
2 Midnight
3 Cavalieros
4 Marguerita
5 Blues
6 Men
7 Boy
8 Life
9 Trial
10 Chi

1 Jessie's
2 Blonde
3 Games
4 Lion's
5 Bachfield
6 Death
7 Fool
8 Castles
9 Bermuda
10 Babes

1 80s
2 Creed
3 Dream
4 Presence
5 Crazy
6 Honour
7 Air
8 Talk
9 Message
10 Mysteries

QUIZ 47   **THE OTHER SIDE OF LOVE**

1 'Careless Whisper' by George Michael
2 'Uptown Girl' by Billy Joel
3 'Freedom' by Wham!
4 'Do They Know It's Christmas?' by Band Aid
5 'Relax!' by Frankie Goes To Hollywood
6 'Two Tribes' by Frankie Goes To Hollywood
7 'The Reflex' by Duran Duran
8 'Wake Me Up Before You Go-Go' by Wham!
9 'We Are The World' by USA For Africa
10 'I Feel Fine' by the Beatles
11 'Call Me' by Blondie
12 '99 Red Balloons' by Nena
13 'Rock Your Baby' by George McCrae
14 'Tainted Love' by Soft Cell
15 'Fernando' by ABBA
16 'Ticket To Ride' by the Beatles
17 'Jumping Jack Flash' by the Rolling Stones
18 'From Me To You' by the Beatles
19 'You Spin Me Round (Like A Record)' by Dead Or Alive
20 'I Don't Like Mondays' by Boomtown Rats

ANSWERS

1. 'Only You' by the Flying Pickets
2. 'Come On Eileen' by Dexy's Midnight Runners
3. 'Happy Talk' by Captain Sensible
4. 'I Feel For You' by Chaka Khan
5. 'Jealous Mind' by Alvin Stardust
6. 'Atomic' by Blondie
7. 'Easy Lover' by Philip Bailey (duet with Phil Collins)
8. 'The Tide Is High' by Blondie
9. 'I Want To Know What Love Is' by Foreigner
10. 'A Little Peace' by Nicole
11. 'Move Closer' by Phyllis Nelson
12. 'Sugar Sugar' by the Archies
13. 'I Should Have Known Better' by Jim Diamond
14. 'One Day In Your Life' by Michael Jackson, and also 'Total Eclipse Of The Heart' by Bonnie Tyler. Two points for each
15. 'Cryin'' by Don MacLean
16. 'Red Red Wine' by U.B.40
17. 'Eye Of The Tiger' by Survivor
18. 'Kung Fu Fightin'' by Carl Douglas, and also 'Puttin' On The Style' by Lonnie Donegan. Two points for each
19. 'In The Summertime' by Mungo Jerry
20. 'Save Your Love' by Renee and Renato

1. 'Give It Up' by KC and the Sunshine Band
2. 'Pass The Dutchie' by Musical Youth
3. 'I've Never Been To Me' by Charlene
4. 'Jealous Guy' by Roxy Music
5. 'Coward Of The County' by Kenny Rogers
6. 'I Got You Babe' by Sonny and Cher
7. 'Knock Three Times' by Dawn
8. 'In The Year 2525' by Zager and Evans
9. 'Dizzy' by Tommy Roe
10. 'When You're In Love With A Beautiful Woman' by Dr Hook
11. 'Video Killed The Radio Star' by Buggles
12. 'Gonna Make You A Star' by David Essex
13. 'We Don't Talk Anymore' by Cliff Richard
14. 'Lucille' by Kenny Rogers
15. 'The Streak' by Ray Stevens
16. 'Waterloo' by ABBA
17. 'One Day At A Time' by Lena Martell
18. 'Sugar Baby Love' by Rubettes
19. 'Welcome Home' by Peters and Lee
20. 'Blockbuster' by Sweet

ANSWERS

QUIZ 48 **COUNTDOWN TO ECSTASY**

1. Beach Boys
2. ABBA
3. AC/DC
4. Adam and the Ants
5. Beatles
6. Bee Gees
7. Black Sabbath
8. Clash
9. Eagles
10. Creedence Clearwater Revival
11. T. Rex
12. Sex Pistols
13. Cliff Richard
14. Elton John
15. Joe Jackson
16. Genesis
17. Marvin Gaye
18. Bob Dylan
19. Pink Floyd
20. Led Zeppelin

QUIZ 49 **BEAUTY AND THE BEAST**

1. Cliff Richard with camel
2. Springfields with Lenny the Lion
3. John Deacon of Queen with Goofy
4. Billy Fury with sheep
5. Fourmost with giraffe

QUIZ 50 **RIDE THE GROOVE**

1. *Chess*, Various Artists
2. *Welcome To The Pleasuredome*, Frankie Goes To Hollywood
3. *The Sound Of Music*, Various Artists
4. *Can't Slow Down*, Lionel Richie
5. *33⅓*, Power Station
6. *Dream Into Action*, Howard Jones
7. *Sergeant Pepper's Lonely Hearts Club Band*, Beatles
8. *The Rise And Fall Of Ziggy Stardust And The Spiders From Mars*, David Bowie
9. *The Works*, Queen
10. *Diamond Life*, Sade
11. *Never Mind The Bollocks Here's The Sex Pistols*, Sex Pistols
12. *Make It Big*, Wham!
13. *Pet Sounds*, The Beach Boys
14. *Nightflight To Venus*, Boney M
15. *The Woman In Red*, Stevie Wonder and Dionne Warwick etc
16. *Let It Bleed*, Rolling Stones
17. *Thriller*, Michael Jackson
18. *Bat Out Of Hell*, Meat Loaf
19. *Rio*, Duran Duran
20. *Human Racing*, Nik Kershaw

ANSWERS

1 *Original Soundtrack*, 10 C.C.
2 *The Secret Of Association*, Paul Young
3 *Songs From The Big Chair*, Tears For Fears
4 *Avalon*, Roxy Music
5 *Steps In Time*, King
6 *Abbey Road*, Beatles
7 *A Tonic For The Troops*, Boomtown Rats
8 *Agent Provocateur*, Foreigner
9 *Break Out*, Pointer Sisters
10 *Electric Warrior*, T. Rex
11 *Faster Than The Speed Of Night*, Bonnie Tyler
12 *Sheer Heart Attack*, Queen
13 *Silver*, Cliff Richard
14 *Innervisions*, Stevie Wonder
15 *Super Trouper*, ABBA
16 *Spirits Having Flown*, Bee Gees
17 *Synchronicity*, Police
18 *Dark Side Of The Moon*, Pink Floyd
19 *The Crossing*, Big Country
20 *Be Yourself Tonight*, Eurythmics

1 *The Distance*, Bob Seger and The Silver Bullet Band
2 *Who's Next*, Who
3 *After The Goldrush*, Neil Young
4 *Jump Up*, Elton John
5 *Makin' Movies*, Dire Straits
6 *Meat Is Murder*, Smiths
7 *Fans*, Malcolm MacLaren
8 *She's The Boss*, Mick Jagger
9 *Life's A Riot With Spy vs Spy*, Billy Bragg
10 *Fate For Breakfast*, Art Garfunkel
11 *Girls Girls Girls*, Elvis Presley
12 *Goat's Head Soup*, Rolling Stones
13 *Bookends*, Simon and Garfunkel
14 *461 Ocean Boulevard*, Eric Clapton
15 *Nashville Skyline*, Bob Dylan
16 *Don't Shoot Me I'm Only The Piano Player*, Elton John
17 *What's Going On*, Marvin Gaye
18 *Exodus* or *Legend*, Bob Marley and the Wailers. Three points for each
19 *A Date With Elvis*, Elvis Presley
20 *Tea For The Tillerman*, Cat Stevens

QUIZ 51 ITS ALL IN THE GAME

1 Vangelis
2 Simon and Garfunkel
3 Survivor
4 Joe South
5 ABBA
6 Wink Martindale and Max Bygraves
7 Tami Lynn
8 Ventures (John Barry also had a minor hit with this title)
9 Silver Convention
10 Wayne Fontana and The Mindbenders
11 Peter Gabriel
12 Lonnie Donegan
13 Amen Corner
14 Intruders
15 Jo Jo Gunne
16 Slade
17 Del Shannon
18 Olivia Newton-John
19 Van Halen
20 St Cecilia

1 Chelsea
2 Liverpool
3 Nottingham Forest
4 Tottenham Hotspur
5 Tottenham Hotspur
6 Scotland's World Cup Team (1974)
7 England's World Cup Team (1970)
8 Scotland's World Cup Team (1978)
9 Scotland's World Cup Team (1982)
10 Everton
11 'It's All In The Game'
12 'Dreadlock Holiday'
13 Roy Harper
14 John McEnroe
15 Cream
16 'Ashes To Ashes' (The Ashes is the trophy for which England play Australia at cricket)
17 'The Tide Is High'
18 Cassius Clay (later Muhammad Ali)
19 'The Name Of The Game'
20 George Best

1 Jumping – 'Jump' was Van Halen's hit and 'Jump (For My Love)' the Pointers'
2 The former was the theme for *Rocky* and the latter for *Rocky III*
3 George McCrae
4 Johnny and The Hurricanes
5 Marathons
6 'Western Movies'
7 They recorded in Olympic Studios, Barnes, London
8 'Snoopy vs The Red Baron'
9 Lulu
10 Neil Diamond
11 'Bicycle Race'
12 'The Pushbike Song'
13 Suzi Quatro
14 Steve Race
15 Cliff Richard
16 The Who
17 Kenny Rogers
18 Ian Whitcomb
19 *Spinout*
20 Barbra Streisand

ANSWERS

QUIZ 52 IF I RULED THE WORLD

1 'Bohemian Rhapsody'
2 The Royal Family
3 'Queen Of Clubs'
4 'King Of The Road'
5 'King'
6 Prince Charles and Diana, Princess of Wales, *The Official BBC Album of the Royal Wedding*
7 Ben E. King
8 'King Creole'
9 'Kings Of The Wild Frontier'
10 'King Of Pain'
11 'Killer Queen'
12 King
13 'Dancing Queen'
14 Jonathan King
15 Evelyn "Champagne" King
16 King Crimson
17 'The Prince'
18 Carole King
19 B. B. King
20 Prince Buster

1 Kingsmen
2 King Trigger
3 Royal Teens
4 'I Might Have Been Queen'
5 *Abbey Road*
6 'Kings And Queens'
7 Prince Rogers Nelson
8 'Queen Of The Hop'
9 'King Tut'
10 'King Midas In Reverse'
11 Otis Redding and Carla Thomas
12 'King Rocker'
13 'Queen Of My Soul'
14 'Little Queenie'
15 'Princess In Rags'
16 'Queen Of Hearts'
17 Solomon King
18 King Curtis
19 Billy Joe Royal
20 Kingston Trio

1 'Queen Of The House'
2 Billy Howard
3 'Pineapple Princess'
4 'Lavender Blue'
5 Kings of Swing Orchestra
6 King Harvest
7 Claude King
8 Four
9 James Darren
10 King Brothers
11 King Floyd
12 'King Of Clowns'
13 Dave King
14 'King Heroin'
15 Gerry Rafferty
16 'The King Is Gone'
17 Bow Wow Wow
18 Saxon
19 Kingsmen (not the same group as in section B, question 1)
20 Ezz Reco and the Launchers with Boysie Grant

QUIZ 53 IT TAKES TWO

1 Garfunkel
2 Cell
3 Fears
4 In The Dark
5 John Oates
6 Renato
7 Dave
8 Womack
9 Simpson
10 Tennille
11 Cher
12 Orville
13 Creme
14 Melle Mel
15 Don Estelle
16 Paul McCartney
17 Stevie Wonder
18 Olivia Newton-John
19 Frederick
20 Tina Turner

ANSWERS

21 Nancy Sinatra and Frank Sinatra	31 Yazoo
22 Buggles	32 Zager and Evans
23 Dave and Ansil Collins	33 Kenny Rogers and Dolly Parton
24 Bing Crosby and Grace Kelly	34 Shaky and Bonnie
25 Elton John and Kiki Dee	35 Black Lace
26 Althia and Donna	36 Dollar
27 Eurythmics	37 Elaine Paige and Barbara Dickson
28 Everly Brothers	38 Baccara
29 Wham!	39 Giorgio Moroder and Phil Oakey
30 Dave Stewart with Barbara Gaskin	40 David Grant and Jaki Graham

1 Lee	21 Peaches and Herb
2 Tropical	22 Peter and Gordon
3 Peoples	23 James and Bobby Purify
4 Tony Meehan	24 Bardo
5 Jonathan	25 Carpenters
6 Vangelis	26 Billy Eckstine and Sarah Vaughan
7 Prudence	27 Caravelles
8 Whitehead	28 Barbra and Neil
9 Stone	29 Esther and Abi Ofarim
10 Johnny	30 Peter Sellers and Sophia Loren
11 William Bell	31 Merseys
12 Michael	32 Bee Gees (yes they were a duo on this hit)
13 Pia Zadora	33 Johnny and Charley
14 James	34 Jeff Beck and Rod Stewart
15 Teddy Johnson	35 Creatures
16 Allen	36 Ferrante and Teicher
17 Earl Scruggs	37 Fame and Price Together
18 Dudley Moore	38 Dick and Deedee
19 Luigi	39 Chad Stuart and Jeremy Clyde
20 John Ford Coley	40 Billy Preston and Syreeta

1 Frank Sinatra
2 Barbra Streisand
3 Marvin Gaye
4 Bing Crosby
5 B. A. Robertson
6 Roberta Flack
7 Doris Day
8 Cliff Richard
9 Julio Iglesias
10 Stan Getz
11 Nino Tempo and April Stevens and Donny and Marie Osmond
12 Inez and Charlie Foxx and Carly Simon and James Taylor
13 Everly Brothers and Glen Campbell and Bobbie Gentry
14 John Travolta and Olivia Newton-John and Hylda Baker and Arthur Mullard
15 Les Paul and Mary Ford and Millican and Nesbitt
16 Lou Rawls
17 Cher
18 Little Eva
19 Margie Hendrix
20 Michael McDonald

ANSWERS

21 Ruth Davis
22 Katie Kissoon
23 Nelson Pigford
24 Mike Vickers
25 Johnny Bristol
26 Marcia
27 Billy Davis Jr
28 Al Verlaine
29 Harry
30 Connie Stevens
31 Lynsey de Paul and Mike Moran
32 Suzi Quatro and Chris Norman
33 Justin Hayward and John Lodge
34 Haysi Fantayzee
35 Harry Belafonte and Odetta
36 Eric Weissberg and Steve Mandel
37 Patience and Prudence
38 Rex Smith and Rachel Sweet
39 Paul and Barry Ryan
40 Chubby Checker and Bobby Rydell

QUIZ 54 A CHANGE IS GONNA COME

1 Adam Faith
2 Ringo Starr
3 Cliff Richard
4 Doris Day
5 Adam Ant
6 Charles Aznavour
7 Pat Boone
8 David Bowie
9 Paul Jones
10 Eric Clapton
11 John Denver
12 David Essex
13 Connie Francis
14 Billy Fury
15 Elton John
16 Engelbert Humperdinck
17 Buddy Holly
18 Brian Jones
19 Jonathan King
20 Boy George

1 Eden Kane
2 Chaka Khan
3 Brenda Lee
4 Billy Idol
5 Bob Dylan
6 Craig Douglas
7 Tommy Steele
8 Peggy Lee
9 Dean Martin
10 Freddie Mercury
11 Gary Numan
12 Elaine Paige
13 Rick(y) Nelson
14 P. J. Proby
15 Bobby Vee
16 Del Shannon
17 Nick Rhodes
18 David Sylvian
19 Sting
20 Bono

1	Donovan	11	Ann-Margret
2	Madonna	12	Green
3	Sade	13	Millie
4	Melanie	14	Oliver
5	Dion	15	Prince
6	Heinz	16	Nena
7	Vangelis	17	Johnny (of the Hurricanes)
8	Toyah	18	Freddie (of the Dreamers)
9	Annette	19	Gerry (of the Pacemakers)
10	Fabian	20	Harvey (of the Moonglows)

P.S. Yes, we know that Nena (see question C 16) is actually the name of the whole group, and that Rogers is not technically part of Prince's surname, so nit-pickers, desist!

QUIZ 55 **BACK IN THE OLD COUNTRY**

1 USA For Africa
2 *Born in the USA*
3 *American Pie*
4 'America'
5 'I'm So Bored With The USA'
6 American Breed
7 'US Male'
8 'Surfin' USA'
9 'Breakfast In America'
10 'American Trilogy'
11 'All The Way From America'
12 'Back In The USA'
13 'American Tune'

1 'American Girl'
2 1974
3 'American Heartbeat'
4 Patrick Juvet
5 'Only In America'
6 *American Beauty*
7 'America'
8 'America'
9 'All American Boy'
10 'Living In The USA'
11 'American Generation'
12 'American City Suite' by Cashman and West
13 'American Music'

1 'American Hearts'
2 'The American'
3 'An American Dream'
4 'America Is My Home'
5 'Americans'
6 'American Boys'
7 'America, Communicate With Me'
8 'Somewhere In America'
9 *American Gothic*
10 'All American Girls'
11 Electric Flag
12 'America The Beautiful'
13 Kate Smith

ANSWERS

QUIZ 56 THE MAGNIFICENT SEVEN

1 Diana – The Temple of Diana at Ephesus
2 Hanging Gardens – The Hanging Gardens of Babylon
3 Jupiter – The Temple of Jupiter at Olympia
4 Nick Rhodes – Colossus of Rhodes
5 Pyramids – Pyramids
6 Lighthouse, sounds like Pharoahs – Pharos of Alexandria
7 Maus – The Mausoleum tomb of King Mausolus of Halicarnassus

The link is the seven wonders of the ancient world

8 Taj Mahal. The Taj Mahal is often referred to as "the eighth wonder of the world"

QUIZ 57 O SUPERMAN

1 Roy Orbison	11 John Oates
2 Billy Ocean	12 Orchestral Manoeuvres In The Dark
3 Des O'Connor	13 'Oh Boy'
4 Jimmy Osmond	14 'Only You'
5 Mike Oldfield	15 An Oscar
6 Tony Orlando	16 Odyssey
7 Yoko Ono	17 'Orville's Song'
8 Donny Osmond	18 'One Night'
9 Gilbert O'Sullivan	19 Ottawan
10 Hazel O'Connor	20 Overlanders

1 Mike Oldfield	12 'Yummy Yummy Yummy'
2 Obernkirchen	13 'Paper Roses'
3 Oliver	14 O'Jays
4 Reg Owen	15 'Mirrors'
5 John Otway	16 Mary O'Brien
6 Ollie and Jerry	17 Outlaws
7 Marmalade	18 'Love Me For A Reason' – Osmonds
8 *Off The Wall*	19 'Oh Pretty Woman'
9 'Oh Well' and 'Oh Diane' (one point each)	20 Rod Stewart reached number six in 1973, Manfred Mann climbed only to number 11 in 1965
10 '007'	
11 One The Juggler	

1 Osibisa	13 Dermot O'Brien
2 Tony Osborne	14 Al Hudson
3 Alan O'Day	15 Orlons
4 Johnny Otis Show	16 Produce a hit single for Roy Orbison
5 Our Daughter's Wedding	17 Mary O'Hara
6 Nine	18 The other three were all the title tracks of hit albums as well
7 One Hundred Ton And A Feather	19 'Oh Oh, I'm Falling In Love Again' by Jimmie Rodgers
8 Andrew Loog Oldham	20 Olympics in 'Western Movies'
9 Orioles	
10 Shirley Owens	
11 Buck Owens	
12 Shadows	

QUIZ 58 **ON BROADWAY**

1 *Evita*, David Essex
2 *Jesus Christ Superstar*, Petula Clark and Yvonne Elliman (both reached number 47)
3 *Carousel*, Gerry and The Pacemakers
4 *Chess*, Murray Head
5 *Dream Girls*, Jennifer Holliday
6 *Song And Dance* or *Tell Me On A Sunday* (the latter is the title of the first half of the former), Marti Webb
7 *West Side Story*, P. J. Proby
8 *Hair*, Fifth Dimension
9 *Rose Marie*, Slim Whitman
10 *Chess*, Elaine Paige and Barbara Dickson
11 *West Side Story*, The Nice
12 *The King And I*, Kenny Ball and His Jazzmen
13 *Song And Dance* or *Tell Me On A Sunday*, Marti Webb
14 *Dear Anyone*, Hot Chocolate
15 *Aladdin*, Cliff Richard and The Shadows
16 *La Cage Aux Folles*, Gloria Gaynor
17 *Sweet Charity*, Shirley Bassey
18 *The Sound Of Music*, Shirley Bassey
19 *Joseph And The Amazing Technicolor Dreamcoat* – the song was never a hit single in the UK
20 *Requiem* by Andrew Lloyd Webber (maybe not strictly a stage show), Sarah Brightman and Paul Miles-Kingston

1 Barry Manilow
2 Elaine Paige, Barbra Streisand
3 P. P. Arnold
4 Jeffrey Daniels (Shalamar)
5 'Oh What A Circus'
6 *Godspell*
7 Louis Armstrong
8 'Hello Dolly'
9 Topol
10 'If I Were A Rich Man'
11 Paul Nicholas
12 *My Fair Lady*
13 Julie Covington
14 'Only Women Bleed'
15 *Evita*
16 Leonard Bernstein and Stephen Sondheim
17 *Variations*
18 Julian Lloyd Webber
19 *Pippin*
20 'You're The One That I Want' was not in the original show but added to the score for the film version

A N S W E R S

1 'People', the others are from *Hair*
2 'Happy Talk', the others are from *The Sound Of Music*
3 'On The Street Where You Live', the others are from *West Side Story*
4 Memory, the others are from *Evita*
5 On The Street Where You Live', the others are from *A Chorus Line*
6 'Edelweiss', Vince Hill, *The Sound Of Music*
7 'One Night In Bangkok', Murray Head, *Chess*
8 'Aquarius'/'Let The Sunshine In', Fifth Dimension, *Hair*
9 'Send In The Clowns', Judy Collins, *A Little Night Music*
10 'Tell Me On A Sunday', Marti Webb, *Tell Me On A Sunday* or *Song And Dance*
11 'Happy Talk', Captain Sensible, *South Pacific*
12 'Stranger In Paradise', Tony Bennett (there were five other hit versions by Eddie Calvert, Don Cornell, Bing Crosby, the Four Aces and Tony Martin, any one of which is acceptable as a correct answer, though Bennett had the number one), *Kismet*
13 'On The Street Where You Live', Vic Damone, *My Fair Lady* (David Whitfield's minor hit would also suffice)
14 'Don't Cry For Me Argentina', Julie Covington, *Evita*
15 Rosemary Clooney, Sammy Davis Jr, Johnnie Ray, Lita Roza
16 'Hey There'
17 *Stop The World I Wanna Get Off*
18 Anthony Newley
19 *Oliver* (the author was Lionel Bart)
20 There wasn't one

QUIZ 59   IT WAS A VERY GOOD YEAR

1	1984	11	1967
2	1983	12	1983
3	1979	13	1964
4	1963	14	1981
5	1985	15	1965
6	1963	16	1976
7	1964	17	1959
8	1965	18	1984
9	1983	19	1973
10	1978	20	1960

1	1958
2	1972
3	1969
4	1977
5	1961
6	1963
7	1980
8	1966
9	1962
10	1980
11	1971
12	1979
13	1975
14	1981
15	1977
16	1954
17	1966
18	1982
19	1972
20	1982

1	1979	11	1981
2	1981	12	1957
3	1961	13	1981
4	1956	14	1965
5	1958	15	1961
6	1964	16	1982
7	1973	17	1973
8	1978	18	1972
9	1960	19	1973
10	1953	20	1964

ANSWERS

MONEY MONEY MONEY

1 David Soul	11 'Wall Street Shuffle'
2 'Penny Lane'	12 'Goldfinger'
3 Dollar	13 Jet Harris and Tony Meehan
4 'Money'	14 Johnny Cash
5 Bay City Rollers	15 'The Ballad Of Bonnie And Clyde'
6 'Gold'	16 Alan Price
7 Jimmy Helms	17 'Can't Buy Me Love'
8 'Band Of Gold'	18 Ruby Winters
9 *Diamond Dogs*	19 'Silver Star'
10 Detroit Emeralds	20 Flying Lizards

1 'Working For The Yankee Dollar'	11 'Easy Money'
2 'Quarter To Three'	12 'Busted'
3 'Pay To The Piper'	13 'Diamond Smiles'
4 'Money In My Pocket'	14 All-Platinum
5 'Bankrobber'	15 'Take That To The Bank'
6 Clyde McPhatter and the Drifters	16 Jewel Akens
7 'Gold'	17 'For What It's Worth'
8 'Penny Arcade'	18 Lloyd Price
9 'Banks Of The Ohio'	19 'Lucy In The Sky With Diamonds'
10 'Offshore Banking Business'	20 'Take The Money And Run'

1 'Dollar In The Teeth'	11 Alvin Cash and the Crawlers
2 'If I Didn't Have A Dime'	12 'Greenback Dollar'
3 'First I Look At The Purse'	13 'Silver Threads And Golden Needles'
4 'Mama Can't Buy You Love'	14 Plastic Penny
5 'Money Won't Change You'	15 'You've Got To Pay The Price'
6 'Pennies From Heaven'	16 'I've Got Five Dollars And It's Saturday Night'
7 Change	17 Neil Diamond
8 Ray Price	18 'The Payback'
9 'More Money For You And Me'	19 Diamonds
10 'The Pay Off'	20 'Let's Spend The Night Together'

NINETEEN EIGHTY-FOUR

1 Adam Ant	11 Smiths
2 John Lennon	12 Smiths
3 Kenny Loggins	13 Siouxsie and the Banshees
4 Cyndi Lauper	14 Sandie Shaw
5 Malcolm McLaren	15 UB 40
6 Bob Marley and the Wailers	16 Elton John
7 Roland Rat Superstar	17 Queen
8 Cliff Richard	18 Art Company
9 Shaky and Bonnie (Stevens and Tyler)	19 Beatles (re-issue of 1964 hit)
10 Feargal Sharkey	20 Scritti Politti

ANSWERS

1	Whitesnake	11	Blancmange
2	Simple Minds	12	Alexei Sayle
3	Loose Ends	13	Ultravox
4	Carol Lynn Townes	14	Various Artists – it is a compilation album series
5	Chris de Burgh	15	Wang Chung
6	Julian Cope	16	Malcolm McLaren
7	Dali's Car	17	Elton John
8	Cool Notes	18	Bluebells
9	Bananarama	19	Van Halen
10	Alarm	20	Eurythmics

1 Amii Stewart
2 'Nobody's Side' by Elaine Paige
3 Colour Field
4 George Michael
5 Elaine Paige (*Cinema*) and Elkie Brooks (*Screen Gems*)
6 One
7 Russ Abbott
8 Aswad
9 Blanco y Negro
10 Everly Brothers
11 None
12 Shalamar (Jeffrey Daniel)
13 In the States, the artist credit was "Wham featuring George Michael"; in the UK, simply "George Michael"
14 Nolans (*not* Cyndi Lauper)
15 Howard Jones
16 'I Feel For You', recorded by Chaka Khan, written by Prince
17 Hank B. Marvin
18 Alphaville, from Germany, had a hit single entitled 'Big In Japan'
19 Nik Kershaw in 'The Riddle'
20 They both have now had hits produced by Mike Batt. Alvin's, in 1984, was 'I Feel Like Buddy Holly'. The Kursaal Flyers hit with 'Little Does She Know' in 1976

ANSWERS

THE SINGER SANG THE SONG

1 Jackie Trent
2 Showaddywaddy
3 Jethro Tull
4 Bobby Freeman
5 Drifters
6 Depeche Mode
7 Mantovani or Ray Martin
8 Sonny Curtis of the Crickets
9 Diana Ross
10 Master Singers
11 Genesis
12 Roger Miller
13 Tracey Ullman
14 Eddie Cochran
15 Billy Fury
16 Co-Co
17 Drifters
18 Adam Ant
19 Amii Stewart or Box Tops
20 Junior
21 Mungo Jerry
22 Cat Stevens
23 Shalamar
24 Style Council
25 Irene Cara
26 Joe Brown
27 USA For Africa
28 Devo
29 Tight Fit
30 Who
31 Gilbert O'Sullivan
32 Electric Light Orchestra

33 Buggles
34 Beatles or Mamas and the Papas
35 George Harrison
36 John Cougar (John 'Cougar' Mellencamp)
37 Ruby Wright
38 Tremeloes
39 Stylistics
40 Cream
41 Joan Regan
42 **ABBA**
43 Marilyn
44 Dr Hook
45 Elvis Costello and the Attractions
46 Elvis Presley
47 Yazoo
48 Steely Dan
49 David Bowie
50 Players Association
51 Cliff Richard or Four Tops or Tommy Edwards
52 Tony Bennett or Harry Secombe
53 Marvin Gaye and Kim Weston
54 Sam Cooke
55 Tom Robinson
56 John Barry, Al Cirola or Clash
57 Laurie Anderson
58 Drifters (never a UK hit)
59 Frank Sinatra
60 **ABBA**
61 Eurythmics (full title is 'Sexcrime (nineteen eighty-four)'
62 Bee Gees

MORE QUESTIONS THAN ANSWERS

If you have breezed through the rest of the quizzes in this book without having to think too deeply, then this final quiz is for you. Between us we have come up with 100 killer questions, some based on facts that were tucked away quietly in some dusty corner of the music press, and others that require a certain amount of lateral thinking to fathom the answers we are looking for. Those of you who sailed through the other quizzes by constantly cheating and looking up the answers will now come unstuck because we haven't printed the answers to these questions.

The first reader to send us a complete list of 100 correct answers, or failing that, the highest score received by 30 June 1986, will qualify for a free copy of each subsequent edition of the *Guinness Book Of British Hit Singles* for life. We also have 50 GRRR level certificates signed by the authors of this book to give to the senders of the 50 best scores. You have until 30 June 1986 to send your answers to:

More Questions Than Answers
Guinness Superlatives Ltd
33 London Road
ENFIELD
Middlesex EN2 6DJ.

After the above date, you can send a large stamped addressed envelope to the above address and we will send you a list of the answers.

Good luck to you all.

1   What Jane Fonda film is likely to be Simon Le Bon's favourite?

2   To which charity did the proceeds from Welsh group The Llan's single go in 1966?

3   Which film starred the man whose chart hit was the B-side of a number one, and the girl who took two film themes to number one and number two respectively?

4   What stage name did the Farina Brothers adopt?

5   What English village has the same name as a bluesman who recorded for Checker Records?

6   The Yardbirds appeared in the David Hemmings/Vanessa Redgrave film *Blow Up*. What was the name of the song they performed?

7   What is the connection between Stephen Duffy and the Thompson Twins?

8   What band consisted of Persh, Bridges, Riviera, Richards and James?

9   Name three DC comics superheroes named in the titles of chart singles

10   In which Elvis Presley film does an Indian princess teach Elvis yoga?

11   What connects Matthews Southern Comfort, Coasters and Royal Guardsmen?

12   Which Detroit group were spoken of by their own congressman, John Conyers Jr, in the 91st US Congress' *Congressional Record*, as follows: "Their involvement is total and sincere, and whether they are communicating with young people on the basketball court, the baseball field, by personal appearances or through their music, the effect has been inspirational to many, and appreciated by all"?

13   Who was in the best position to know that Esther and Abi Ofarim's 'Cinderella Rockefella' was a gas?

14   Whose first book was called *Tarantula?*

15   By the Spring of 1985, Suzi Quatro had two of them, Cilla Black had three, Alison Moyet almost had one, but Elaine Paige and Barbara Dickson had none, either together or solo. What are they?

16   Which US number one single has a dedication to "B.J.K."?

17   Which artist was the first to be awarded a gold disc?

18   Who was born in an upstairs room in Blackpool?

19   What connects the records of Dexy's Midnight Runners, Rita Coolidge and the Commodores?

20   Which UK number one had original lyrics about the repeal of Prohibition in December 1933 but in its hit form dealt with one man's more personal experience?

21   Omitting one letter from the title of what hit would leave Ben E. King expressing inordinate love for the Little Mermaid?

22   What is the link between Ringo Starr, Nilsson, Elton John and David Bowie?

23   Which recorded prediction of the birth of Louise Brown missed by 4587 years?

24   What major change did L. A. Gaines undergo apart from a name change?

25   If going to a film together, Jerry Dammers and Gene Pitney might well choose one with music by what composer?

26   What is the link between Tony Hatch and Sonny and Cher?

27   Who played "everything apart from the drums" on 'Memo From Turner' by Mick Jagger, according to Jagger himself?

28 Who sold over a million copies of his first hit in 1957 on a label that had not actually signed him, enabling another company to move in and sign him for a spell that produced 30-odd hit singles in under six years?

29 Who is the only artist to have number one hits as a soloist and as a member of a duo, trio, quartet and quintet?

30 Who said in 1970 "What do they expect us to do – drink dewdrops out of rose petals"?

31 Why were Phil Collins, Ferrante and Teicher and Soft Cell all inspired in the same book, and what book is it?

32 Banjo player Erik Darling led the Tarriers into the British and American charts with 'Banana Boat Song'. What was Darling's next world-wide hit?

33 As an active touring band, U2 have flown scores of times. Why else might they be familiar with music for airports?

34 Which former Radio One and Radio Caroline DJ did a race commentary on a Slade album?

35 What was not respectable about the Rolling Stones' 20th British hit single?

36 Apart from the Elaine Paige/Barbra Streisand chart entries how has Cats appeared on the UK charts?

37 What sport would Berry Gordy and Jean Terrell, Diana Ross's replacement in the Supremes, be most likely to discuss?

38 After having many hits and topping the chart with his group, he left and released a solo single 'Aggravation'. Who is he?

39 Which hit song that inspired hundreds of imitative hits was first released as the B-side of the composer's single, 'Teardrops On Your Letter', in 1959?

40 Which Top Ten smash (this side of the Atlantic) has as its flipside 'Stars Fell On Stockton'?

41 What was the only year in the period 1952–84 in which the top two songs on Christmas Day were actually about Christmas?

42 Which number one single of the early 60s featured Lisa Gray on heavenly soprano backing vocals?

43 Who recorded the Buffalo Springfield tune, 'For What It's Worth' with lyrics adapted to make it an anti-blood sports song?

44 Which massive 60s instrumental hit was originally titled 'Jenny'?

45 What male vocalist received label credit in Britain for a hit sung in fact by his wife, who received no credit at all?

46 What is the link between Bob Dylan, Chicken Shack, Association and Neil Young?

47 Why does Los Angeles owe San Francisco the money for the flowers?

48 Why did Dr Hook and the Medicine Show's 1972 US hit 'The Cover of Rolling Stone' never have a chance of hitting the UK charts?

49 What Motown hit featured chirping birds and thunder?

50 Who "passed the hound dog singers home" in their 13th British hit?

51 What chart coincidence makes Go West, ABC and Dead Or Alive different from Duran Duran, Tears For Fears and Kajagoogoo?

52 How do the heirs of Ronnie Mack benefit from a tribute to God?

53 The success of what number one ensured that a song about to be dropped from a Broadway-bound musical was kept in the show?

54 Which Radio One controller wrote the lyrics for Ruby Murray's 1955 chart topper 'Softly Softly' under the pseudonym of Mark Pau?

55 Jackie Wilson and Ben E. King both replaced the same man as lead singer in two different groups. Who was the man and which were the groups?

56 What do the Goffin/King songs 'The Locomotion' and 'Go Away Little Girl' have in common (apart from the fact they are Goffin/King songs, of course)?

57 Who is the only act to chart twice with singles named after itself?

58 What is the link between Marillion, Ricky Nelson and Mezzoforte?

59 Who is or was Mars Bonfire?

60 Which girl group was led by Mary Aliese?

61 Who enjoyed Britain's 503rd number one hit?

62 What achievement do the Specials share with Demis Roussos?

63 Who said, in an interview with *Ebony* magazine: "The first records to really knock me out were 'Don't Roll Those Bloodshot Eyes At Me' by Wynonie Harris and 'Sam Jones Done Snagged His Braces' by Louis Jordan. I knew from then that someday I just had to try and sing like that"?

64 What was the hit single inspired by the American daytime soap opera – *The Young And The Restless*?

65 Repeated plays on *The Muppet Show* helped make what Italian song a Top Ten hit?

66 What is the link between Colour Field, Madness, Bo Diddley, Jilted John, Immaculate Fools and Starvation?

67 Which number one hit writer, better known as a performer although he never had a hit single in Britain, died of Huntington's Chorea?

68 Which two members of which major recording act were part of a group called Smile which had one single released in the States in 1969?

69 Who links Julio Iglesias, Waylon Jennings and Dionne Warwick?

70 A song began life as the B-side of a single by an American act, Raindrops, and was then recorded by two or three other acts, at first all unsuccessfully. One version was played by an East Coast disc jockey over two years later, and then quickly rose to number one in America. What was the song, and who were the Raindrops?

71 Who produced 'I'm Just A Boy' by Deke Arlon and the Offbeats in 1964?

72 Why is Tom Robinson's hit 'Glad To Be Gay' not found in his list of hits?

73 Who released the Beatles song 'I'll Cry Instead' under the alias Vance Arnold in America in 1964?

74 Why did Amanda Parsons and Ann Rosenthal miss the party?

75 What charity did the number two UK hit entitled 'All Star Hit Parade', which featured Dickie Valentine, Joan Regan, Winifred Atwell, Dave King, Lita Roza and David Whitfield benefit in 1956?

76 The melody of Chuck Berry's 'Sweet Little Sixteen' returned to the chart five years later as the tune of what hit?

77 On the album *End Of The Century* the Ramones played a track called 'Do You Remember Rock 'n' Roll Radio'? (also a UK single). One line of the song asked "Do you remember Jerry Lee, John Lennon, T. Rex and ole Moulty"? The first three are familiar but which American garage band did Moulty drum for and what was so significant about him?

78 Which song did Bob Dylan write in honour of a baseball pitcher?

79 How many of Cliff Richard's singles were issued in the UK on 78 rpm?

80 A supergroup consisting of Johnny Rotten on lead vocals, Phil Manzanera on guitar, Paul McCartney on bass and Elton John on keyboards might well be produced by whom?

81 The record 'Let's Go To San Francisco' was recorded by a group of session musicians called the Flowerpot Men. After it became a hit a more permanent band was formed to go on tour Who played keyboards with this band with which group did he find greater success?

82 Who said, "That Elvis man, he is all there is. There ain't no more. Everything starts and ends with him. He wrote the book"?

83 Which chart artist of the 70s and 80s was once backed by the Blue Monks?

84 Why was Paul Young fortunate to have a copy of the original hit version of 'Too Busy Thinking About My Baby'?

85 Who was the pianist on Cat Steven's hit version of 'Morning Has Broken'?

86 What were Michael Haslam and Bob Bain doing in Walthamstow on 24 October 1964?

87 Which successful California band absorbed members of an unsuccessful band called The Brogues?

88 His real name was Bent Fabricus Bjerre and his pen name was Frank Bjorn. What was his million-selling Grammy-winning single?

89 What characteristic was shared by Curved Air's first LP and Daryl Way's violin?

90 What did Earl Vance and the Valiants give up in February 1971?

91 When was Gary Glitter a priest?

92 What number one hitmaker would Nick Tosches and Myra Lewis most likely discuss?

93 Which song plays on the radio at the start of the film *Road Movie*?

94 What song was written for a TV Programme that also featured a Canadian swimmer narrowly failing to break a world record, and what was the programme called?

95 Which British recording act scored their 10th hit in 10 releases with a disc whose 12-inch version contained two tracks entitled 'Coalmines' and 'We Fall'?

96 What chart act could have contained Maybelle Carter, Earl Hines, Janet Mead and Jack McDuff?

97 Who were led by Bo Winberg?

98 To what artist was the line "Success is nothing without someone you love to share it with" important?

99 Which Eurovision Song Contest entry has been the most successful (to 1985) in the American charts?

100 Who has written or co-written an American number one every year from 1978 to 1985?

HITS CHALLENGE FIRST EDITION

Those readers wishing to receive a list of the answers to *Hits Challenge First Edition* 'More Questions Than Answers' can do so by writing to the Publishers at the following address:

GUINNESS SUPERLATIVES Ltd
33 London Road,
Enfield, Middlesex EN2 6DJ

Please send a large stamped addressed envelope.